Price
Life's a Pitch.

"Soni's approach is elegant, gracious, and graceful. This is a must read for anyone serious about their profession and success. You will love this book!"

Marsha Petrie Sue, Award Winning Author of The CEO of YOU
Past President of the National Speakers Association—Arizona

"Soni's enthusiasm for her work is infectious and her ability to make even the shyest of souls shine is unmatched!"
Maura Donley, Vice President of Membership and Communications
Pennsylvania Chamber of Business and Industry

"Energy, energy, energy! That's Soni Dimond. Five minutes with her and you're fired up and ready to go. Her training sessions keep everyone focused and allow even typically shy people to come out of their shells. They gain confidence and begin to communicate effectively. I've seen it happen!"

Steven P. Buterbaugh, Vice President
E.K. McConkey & Co., Inc. Insurance

"I have been privileged to work with Soni on many occasions in showing entrepreneurs how to present their companies effectively. It is a real treat to see their faces light up as she proves to them that substance without style is an ineffective way to sell an idea."
Michael L. Hund, Esq., Shareholder and Co-chair
Venture Capital and Emerging Companies Practice Group
Buchanan Ingersoll, PC

"Soni Dimond will entertain, motivate, and enrich your life. She's energetic and mesmerizing, so be prepared to pay attention. You won't want to miss a word because everything she has to say is important to you, personally and professionally. Best of all, she makes it fun!"

Linda Drake, President
National Verbatim Reporters Association

"Soni brings wisdom and wit to her presentations—a style reflected in her book which, simply put, provides a prescription for success for those of us in the public eye."

John A. Garner, Jr., Executive Director
Pennsylvania League of Cities & Municipalities

"Soni's experience and enthusiasm enabled her to connect with our students and provide them with the networking skills to begin their professional careers."

Dr. Anthony S. Winter, Associate Dean and Business Internship Director
John L. Grove College of Business, Shippensburg University

"The Greater Philadelphia Chamber of Commerce has hosted several of Soni's programs. They always sell out and we receive great feedback. People come to see her again and again because she always has new information and delivers it with such captivating energy. Everyone leaves with skills they can practice immediately. We love working with her."

Lisa Hahn, Manager
Programs & Events, Greater Philadelphia Chamber of Commerce

"Soni Dimond is fantastic. Her energy, enthusiasm, and knowledge are contagious. I've worked with a lot of trainers and Soni is right at the top of the list. She's been there and done that and anyone can benefit from her experience."

Kenneth E. Lawrence, Jr., President
Public Affairs Strategies
Formerly, Manager of Public Affairs, Merck & Company, Inc.

"Soni Dimond is all the things you'd want in a radio guest: smart, informative, and entertaining. It's been great working with her!"

Marc Miranda, Producer
"Person to Person with Matt Gerson," KXAM Radio 1310 AM
Phoenix, Arizona

"I have been blessed with watching Soni grow up for twenty-five years. She has a professional program designed to take up where your mother left off."

Wendy A. David, Executive Vice President
Home Builders Association, Metropolitan Harrisburg

"Soni instills humor into every corner while teaching valuable lessons and skills with panache!"

Wanda D. Filer, MD, President
Strategic Health Institute

"The reality here is Soni delivers sophisticated commentary and media relations empowerment. Without a doubt, her pitch is true and straight." *Life's a Pitch!*™ is already a favorite in my office."

Beth Winters, Executive Director and General Counsel
Drug Free Pennsylvania

"Soni Dimond has been entertaining and educating readers of *We* magazine since 2002. She provides the smarts we all need to be successful and savvy communicators."

Fran Lowe, Executive Editor
We magazine

"*Life's a Pitch!*™ is a great opportunity for early stage tech companies to sharpen their message to investors and key customers. The investment up front in this session pays great dividends when you consider the end result can be sales closed faster and venture capital secured."

Jennifer Hammaker, President
Yellowcakes, Inc.

"Soni helped our clients become much more polished in preparing to make pitches to investors. *Life's a Pitch!*™ makes selling a clear and straightforward process by explaining what your audience or customer hears and how they interpret it."

Jill Edwards, Executive Director
Ben Franklin Venture Investment Forum

LIFE'S A PITCH!™

From Hosting to Toasting . . .
From News to Schmooze

SONI DIMOND

To order additional copies of this book, contact:
Xlibris Corporation
1-888-795-4274 Ext. 276, 24 hours
www.Xlibris.com
Orders@Xlibris.com
You are welcome to contact us at www.sonidimond.com with questions about
ordering.
25411

Dedication

This book is dedicated to Kevin Martorana.

Without you . . . I wouldn't be me.

CONTENTS

PART ONE
Pitch with Panache

The art of courteous, considerate conversation and
behavior in any setting; topics include verbal,
email, and other interactions

Selecting the proper attire for special occasions;
topics include Black and White Tie attire for ladies
and gentlemen and suitable accessories

Dining protocol and related social graces for hosts
and guests; topics include gracious hosting, table
manners, and various uses of utensils and plates

Telephone etiquette; topics include attitude, tone,
voicemail, and cell phone use for callers and recipients

PART TWO
Pitch Like a Pro! From Job Interviews to Social Schmooze

PART THREE
Enrich Your Pitch

Gaining the skills to enjoy public speaking; topics
include the essentials of preparation, appearance,
delivering the message, credibility, the value of
rehearsing, and respecting the audience

Combatting stage fright with "Fluster Busters";
topics include common physical effects and how
to deal with them, how to engage the audience to
help you relax, and how the show can go on even
under stage fright's spell

Working with electronic and print media
successfully; topics include determining news
vs. ads, knowing what various media needs in a
news pitch, respecting media professionals' time
schedules, and presenting the proper pitch for
newsworthy stories

PART FOUR
The Ceremonial Pitch

Delivering and receiving toasts at special occasions;
topics include the preparation required of hosts
and toasters, writing and presenting the toast,
appropriate acknowledgements and timing

FOREWORD

Welcome and congratulations! You have invested in maximizing your success.

As a respected member of the National Speakers Association and voted one of the Best 50 Women in Business by the Pennsylvania Department of Community and Economic Development, Soni Dimond is about to guide you through the importance of presenting yourself with protocol, sharpening your self promotion, developing your positive image, networking with a purpose, managing your media message, and the success that directly results from honing these skills. Whether you are an entrepreneur, employee, student, corporate executive, or simply breathing the air, she gives you a unique look at being memorable. This is a collection of practical ways to make a positive, outstanding impression in a world filled with clutter, information overload, and occasional chaos.

No other book is quite this. Soni supplies field tested skills, pitching you high above the competition, time and time again.

You will:

◊ Climb beyond the anxiety of public speaking and news interviews
◊ Land the job of your dreams and make more money
◊ Converse even in the most difficult circumstance and save time doing it
◊ Maximize every telephone interface and ignite the call to action

◊ Self promote without sounding like an infomercial
◊ And much, much more!

She is about to help you understand that knowledge is not power, *application* is. The challenge? Have a strong belief in yourself, your services, your products, and what you have to share with the world. Be prepared to strut your stuff and be at your best. Then, deal with the rest. After all, Life's a Pitch!

Happy Reading!

Marsha Petrie Sue

As an award-winning author and international speaker, Marsha Petrie Sue, MBA and former corporate executive, is a leadership and professional development expert. She works with companies that want to inspire change to improve productivity and profits. www.MarshaPetrieSue.com

INTRODUCTION

Pitch, pitch, pitch. We do it every day. We "sell" ourselves silly in so many ways: from hosting a party to toasting a wedding; from landing a new job to leading a Board of Directors meeting; from working a room filled with colleagues to conducting a broadcast interview; from addressing a convention to addressing a letter, and more.

How do *you* "sell" yourself to others? Are you making the best possible impression? It's unfair really, but attitudes and appraisals can be affected by how you sell your most precious commodity—*yourself!*

First, try a soft pitch by working your soft skills: your interpersonal skills and strengths. You may think these abilities don't matter much. Soft skills don't sound strong and measurable. So who needs them? The answer is *you* do. Their value is often beyond measure. They're within every one of us, yet are sometimes conspicuous by their absence. My goal in writing *Life's a Pitch!™* is to help you seek out and sharpen your soft skills. I'm pleased to assist you in shining a light on your inner strengths.

Be your best, personally, every day. From new friends to newfound influence, you'll see the results in many ways.

Professionally, you can translate your softer interpersonal talents into hard, strong, quantifiable numbers when it comes to landing a job, negotiating a salary, or being recognized as an expert in your field.

Executives and other professionals in corporations and associations, as well as small business owners and high-profile individuals, trust me on a weekly basis to coach them in communication skills. Together, we present their most pertinent messages and their most polished images to their targeted audiences. Entrepreneurs seeking venture capital have drawn upon my services, and after applying new techniques, have enhanced their abilities to seek much-needed investment money for their innovative inventions or concepts.

It takes energy and initiative to self-promote. It takes bravery, talent, and finesse, too. I applaud each and every person who gives it a try. Preparation and persistence are the secrets to public speaking success. Conversely, lack of knowledge is noticeable—and can be costly.

Those who are in the know, know to seek training.

I came across this need for presentation training when I worked in the public affairs arena in Washington, D.C. Sometimes, amazingly, the highest ranking individual had the lowest self-esteem. I learned the art of providing classic media training when I was called upon to place these newsmakers on network television or in newspapers and magazines. I allowed my clients to hear and see themselves deliver their messages. They soon realized the power of video playback.

When I ran the media relations department at the Pennsylvania Chamber of Business and Industry, the Commonwealth's largest broad-based business association, I continued to coach others to rehearse with the help of a video camera. Some of the most astonishing words have come out of our members' mouths, from sheer delight ("I am more effective than I thought I was!") to utter determination ("I can do better than that! Let me try again!").

Often, members of our phenomenal Board of Directors at this distinguished, high-profile Chamber needed guidance to control their messages when faced with reporters' interviews. Our government affairs specialists and business advocates needed the power to persuade when lobbying for new legislation. Most already knew how to do this quite well. Yet, with an open mind and a bit of gentle guidance, even the most polished business leaders, some of whom controlled billions of dollars, discovered how to increase their clout with effective communication.

To my delight, in the late 1990's, I discovered I had a knack for assisting individuals in facing the podium fearlessly, pitch their message powerfully, and present themselves appropriately. I started training executives, and found they enjoyed the process as much as I did. In fact, for me, it became a life-changing experience. I caught the entrepreneurial bug.

Soon, I left my day job and launched my own communications and public relations business, Soni Dimond Media. I started my business by playing to my strengths and doing what I had been doing for others: news publicity and promotion. Immediately, in support of my business venture, and much to my delight, the Pennsylvania Chamber signed on as my first client! There was no turning back. I negotiated that first client. Now I was committed to succeed.

During my first month in business, my photo and story titled "Harrisburg's Spinmeisters" appeared on the cover of *Harrisburg Magazine*. The publication named my firm among the best in their readership area. It seems my business has been on the "Spin Cycle" ever since!

I'm pleased to say that my clients have ranged in age from 12 to 102 and in aptitudes and talent from a child prodigy pianist to a potato chip producer. They include a million-dollar quiz show winner, a seven-foot, furry theme park mascot, and leaders of Fortune 500 corporations. I've trained politicians, doctors, lawyers, and a rabbi. (I know there's a joke in there, somewhere!) One thing they've all had in common is the need to "Be aware, be sincere, be your best"©. To pitch with power and self-promote with style, they've needed a best friend, a confidante, or perhaps a careful critic.

When I accompany a client to a high-profile venue, such as *Oprah*, or if my client appears in *People* magazine, I am reminded that our hard work has opened doors to producers, editors, and decision makers. If their message is noteworthy, I help my clients make all levels of media interested in their pitch.

It is my belief that these "soft" communications skills are not usually taught in schools today. I am ready and willing to visit schools to share the knowledge students will need to communicate and compete in their adult lives. I have been honored to participate in media literacy campaigns, such as *The Media Straight Up! "Critical Thinking Skills for Pennsylvania's Youth,"* hosted by Drug Free Pennsylvania.

Among other skill builders, I have coached teachers to help students determine the difference between a well-written paid ad and a well-earned news story. These teachers learned the protocol of media mobilization and contacts as well as the guidelines to help students produce their own public service announcements. *Life's a Pitch!™* pinpoints useful media tips, tactics, and strategies in Chapter 12, "Toss a Good News Pitch."

To help others with survival tactics for social and professional situations, I've been honored to draft my monthly column in *We* magazine. Since our need for communication runs the gamut of gab, and because so many individuals need to address the public, I've dubbed the piece "News, Views, Muse and Schmooze." Designed as an easy reader, it addresses our everyday communications challenges . . . with a chuckle.

It seems that someone somewhere started the rumor that public speaking should be regarded as a fear worse than death. I'm here to share this with you: it is quite the opposite. Here's the secret: most people already have the strengths they need to pitch their best talents and "sell" themselves. We do it daily in our personal interactions, with family affairs, and at social functions. So, relax. Public speaking and personal presentation are actually much easier than you might think.

Fortunately, I have picked up some great tips from people who know a lot more than I. I am sure my colleagues at the National Speakers Association would agree: if we stop talking *to* people and start talking *with* them, we can learn more from others every day. Doesn't it feel more satisfying when someone says, "Nice talking *with* you . . ." instead of, "Nice talking *to* you . . ."?

Use this book. There's a wealth of fundamental information

and fun facts I want to share. A lot of it you'll know, some of it you'll learn, and I hope all of it, you'll like. You can read it front to back or back to front. Select and use the tips you find interesting peppered throughout. Much like life, it has its unexpected surprises along with humorous moments and serious messages. Like life, you *gotta* laugh sometimes at the ironies and the absurdities. And you *gotta* laugh at yourself. All you really need are "in"sights to the perfect pitch: interest, inflection, instincts, initiative, intuition, and intriguing social and professional behavior.

In *Life's a Pitch!*™, I hope to help guide you, your colleagues, your sons, and daughters through the fine points of soft skills. In this book, I address how to dine with proper etiquette, what to wear and say at a job interview, and how to send a memorable thank you note. I also want people of all ages learn to appreciate the value of effective networking. If you do it the right way, you can meet a new friend, land a new job, or seal a sweet business deal. Networking is so much more than a handshake or small talk. It's a dealmaker or a dealbreaker. Check out Chapter 8 "Your Personal Sales Pitch" for some tips so you don't lose your schmooze.

You can publicize your inherent skills to others in so many ways. In addition to learning how to be gracious and grateful, discover how to be the "Most Valuable Player" in social gatherings and business settings!

Allow me to join your fans, cheering you on as you train to pitch your strengths, promote yourself, your cause, or your business. Throw your marvelous message out there! This book can make it easier, and I'll bet you'll have fun doing it.

ACKNOWLEDGMENTS

Winners know you can't pitch a winning game without a solid team. I am in awe of the team of tremendous talent who made this book become a reality.

To my husband, Kevin Martorana, my gratitude goes beyond thanks . . . for your encouragement and compassion during the pursuit of my writing passion. You must know how much I love you. Let me tell you again.

A huge hug goes to Stacey Hanby, my guardian angel, simply disguised as my business associate. I thank you from my heart. With countless personal qualities and your amazing character, you're the most gracious person I know. Even when I'm testing your limits, you remind me "that's just not attractive." Thanks for being my role model. When I grow up I want to be just like you. So glad we found each other.

To Kathy King, my "Detail Diva" and devoted "To Do" task mistress, thank you for compiling and organizing my many articles and for tolerating my ambitious agenda. Thank you, too, for bending . . . on my use of the ellipsis.

To "Jazzy" Carol Jones, thank you for being my designing woman. I'm sending admiration and appreciation for this book's cover as well as our many magazine ads.

I offer my sincere appreciation to all of the women who founded and forged ahead with *We* magazine, the birthplace of this book.

Great gratitude goes to Donna Angelillo, Liz Maneval, Fran Lowe, and Barbara (Babs) Kyne. You have allowed me to create *Life's A Pitch!™* from my many ramblings in "News, Views, Muse and Schmooze." Thank you dahlings for giving me the freedom to express—in 1,000 words or less!

Special thanks, on both personal and professional levels, goes to my National Speakers Association (NSA) guru gals, "Marvelous" Marsha Petrie Sue from Arizona and "High-Speed" Heshie Segal, the "JetNetter" from Pennsylvania. I have Marsha Davis to thank for introducing me to the marvels of NSA's Mid-Atlantic Chapter.

A big Arizona appreciation goes to Charlotte Hodel, who put her heart and soul into bringing "Dimond to the Desert."

To my dahling*est* "Fancy Nancy" Hoover, my runnin' buddy who volunteers her valuable "Meeting Maven" talents for the thrill of the road. You have taught me what friends are for, and for that, I love *you* more!

For providing a safe shore for my shipping, I thank our extended office, the terrific team at the UPS Store, Bob, Trish, Jared, and Teresa. You have kept tabs on the progress of this book since the beginning of the business. Thanks for being there when I needed you.

Cheers to my clients and friends (some are one and the same) who have put their early faith in my work. A toast to you!

To Lew Ebert, thanks for giving "The Sonmeister" her first Chamber job.

Powerful appreciation is sent to Floyd Warner, Maura Donley, and *all* of my colleagues, professional and personal, at the Pennsylvania Chamber of Business and Industry. No matter where I go, all roads lead back to you.

I will never forget Vic Russo, Steve Brawley and all of the wonderful people at the Ben Franklin Technology Partners, including "Generous" Jen Hammaker, who now heads Yellowcakes, but started the Ben ball rolling. This profitable contact emerged within the first few hours of launching my firm. I'm happy to say, we're still doing good work. Our relationships have prospered and paralleled from personal to professional since day one.

To all the chambers of commerce, professional associations, businesses, public officials, news editors and advertising execs, radio hosts and TV talents, emcees, producers, and individuals of all ages and walks of life with whom I've worked. I have been honored to serve with you. Special thanks to former "Fabulous" Harrisburg Magazine Publisher Carol Morris and Editor "Extraordinaire" Lisa Paige. I'll never forget my first. That includes my first media training session and my original *tasteful* clients, such as Herr Foods Inc., a sensational snack food company!

I'm thankful for "Susan K" Kessler, who allowed me to take her fashion flair to TV, and to Barry "The Baron" Kessler who convinced me that a "delightfully different" life would await me if I only had the guts to be my own boss. Hugs to Ty McCauslin. Kisses to former "Susan K-ers," Kathy and Kay, who babysat the baby biz. Oh how we've grown!

Thanks to Cindy Foster of the PA League of Cities and Municipalities for making me a league "regular."

Special sentiments go out to Sam Apicelli, who protects my intellectual property, entertains all the new ideas I send his way, but trademarks *only* the good ones.

To Deborah Brandt, I am blessed to know you. You are responsible for SDM's custom look. I cherish our yearly quest to design each new batch of SDM collectible cards.

To anyone who has ever graced me with the gift of friendship, I'm grateful for your presence in my life. Here's to our stolen moments.

To my phenomenal family I owe everything . . .

To Pat and Ken Dimond, thank you for believing your daughter could conquer the world. You may think you are my biggest fans, but I am yours.

To Kendra Dimond, who tolerated me as your little sister, then took me as a grown-up partner to the national podium, from Washington, D.C. to Boston—I thank you for believing in me as much as I believe in you.

To Elena, who told me I "Shoulda! Coulda! Woulda!"© long ago, I thank you for encouraging your Auntie.

To my father-in-law, Dominic Martorana, you know this book would not be possible without your loving support.

To Joan Simmons, a sincere thank you for your swift and silly sense of humor . . . *no matter what!*

To anyone who laughs at the title of this book but who takes my work seriously, be assured, I am grateful.

From inspiration to perspiration to anticipation, *Life's A Pitch!™* has been a delightful journey.

LIFE'S A PITCH!™

PART ONE

Pitch with Panache

CHAPTER 1

Speak Your Mind
Or Bite Your Tongue

P ardon me. May I have a moment? Your etiquette slips may be showing.

This book is about communication, yet it's essential to take time to remind ourselves of the exceptional value of uncommon courtesy. From discussion to demeanor to dress, manners matter.

Most of us agree, in today's times, our traditional good manners have been underestimated. Some people regard protocol as purely incidental in the grand scheme of things. It is true that politeness may be irrelevant to some. Give yourself the edge by practicing your politeness and proper behavior.

Good manners are so rare and so cherished that people will reward you for your effort in both social and business venues. This requires work and attention. Remember the kind, courteous person you are? Practice your good manners with sincerity and generosity of spirit. Be aware, be sincere, be your best©. No one likes to be tricked into falling for a phony.

Where to start? Be proactive, not reactive. Turn the attention away from yourself. Respect other people. Focus on others' accomplishments and applaud their generosity and spirit. This will help you make good first *and lasting* impressions. By making others more comfortable in conversation and other situations, you will be remembered fondly later, with a smile.

Ever think of someone and smile? Then they made a great impression on you.

How rude! Desiring those days of polite conversation and discreet discussion.

What's considered polite conversation these days? Can you recall days of good manners and decorum? Remember when the rules were defined oh, so clearly? Not anymore. Chances are, we encounter rudeness, or we're guilty of being rude, every busy, frenetic, emailing, cell phone using, voicemail answering, multitasking day. Do you feel you're getting so rattled that you could easily become rude? When stressed, handle your communications with care.

Why is it so hard to be gentle? We recognize it may be getting difficult to mind our manners while minding our demanding schedules. If you are having a bad day, learn to avoid transferring your emotions into your speech. This takes some effort. We know too well that there's a thin line between *a*nger and *d*anger. It's as simple as adding one letter, as the saying goes.

Are you aware of your choice of words and how they may sound to others? In conversations as well as in voice and email, once your words have been "sent," you usually cannot "retrieve" or "delete" them. It makes good sense to use our senses. If we are blessed with hearing, we must learn to listen. If we can see, we must examine ourselves from another perspective so we may consider how others see us. We must be familiar with how to cope with our range of feelings and play nice. Learn the joys of being polite in life, in love, and in social interactions.

Say what?

People remember the very good and the very bad things others say to them. Even in emotional conversations, think of your words as quotes attributed to you. If you are angry about something, resist leaving a heated message on voicemail. Avoid sending email until you are certain you can stand behind those words. Examine that email. Read it carefully *before* you hit the "Send" button. How would you react if someone sent you an email like the one you might have drafted? Perhaps you'd like to tone it down or not put those mean-spirited thoughts in writing. People may forgive, but they often do not forget rude language. So pause a moment before you take action. Write and speak as if you are being quoted. You probably will be.

Scowl and the world frowns with you.

In most cultures, there's no room for rude behavior. Being impolite is considered extremely ugly behavior, and well, who wants to be ugly? So don't lower your standards. No one will be impressed if they see you making the nasty faces necessary to utter unpleasant words. It's unbecoming. To check your expressions, try this: stand at a mirror and say a few pleasant phrases such as, "How nice of you to think of me," or "What an interesting idea." Now say the same phrases with sarcasm in your voice. Do you see what happens to your face? I think we must agree. It's just not appealing. You may think your caustic humor is witty but you are only being nasty, and sadly, nasty people look the part.

Dimond's Gems

There's no such thing as a good whine.

"Whines" do not improve with age.

It's safe to say, most of us are capable (and we may believe we're deserving) of indulging in a whine. Children, and those who don't know any better, may be forgiven. Yet, we know that *you* do know better.

Think you have troubles? Get in line! Most of us have something in our lives to complain about. So let's buck up and stop the fuss. No one wants to hear it. Why in the world would they? Whining is all about you and that means it is not respectful of others. You'll be more respected and you may find solutions to your problems as soon as you lose that "woe is me" mentality. Avoid anguishing over situations you cannot control. Instead, acknowledge the absurdity of whining. Laugh about it, if you can. Think of solutions and common-sense approaches to your predicament.

Yes, there are times each one of us needs to vent. So just blow off that steam by commiserating with a friend. Keep it brief and nonpublic. Afterward, put a cork in it and move on!

Some cell phone use requires solitary confinement.

A polite reminder to our readers . . . *We can hear you now!* In public places, chances are, those who are around you may hear every word of your cell phone conversation. So, when you must talk on your cell phone, try to step away from crowds, if possible. You may not know how loudly you're actually speaking when on your cell. It is important to tell your cell phone callers where you are so they can adjust and expect any interruption or distraction. Respect public "quiet zones" and "cell phone-free sections" in libraries, museums, schools, places of worship, and the growing popularity of "quiet cars" on trains.

Flush out that potty mouth.

"*?&^X#&^/#*@#!!*" If you just hit your thumb with a hammer, or if you just spilled hot coffee on your lap, we can *almost* forgive you for saying that.

Yet, if something is upsetting you, a good rule is: cope with it; don't curse at it. Perhaps you think it's far too simple to slip and bellow out a swear word because you say it feels good. To whom? To you! What about those around you? When you swear out loud, you are not respecting others. It's just not polite.

Think about the damage that word could cause. The next time you find yourself tempted to employ an expletive, consider some R & R: Replacing & Rephrasing. Oops! Too late to rephrase? Already let the words out? Then stop and apologize to those around you. What replacement word could have been used to tame the tone of what you said? Next time, you may choose to switch your word to that selection. You are smart enough to know you can still make your point, but with composure and class.

Don't mistake niceness for weakness.

Afraid if you're too polite you'll be considered weak? A truly polite person is strategic about the selection of words, tone, and venue. A polite person knows better than to visit topics, persons, or places that could lead to potential contention. If that means you must develop a neutral tone instead of your typical lively inflection, then so be it. No need to be rude. It won't make you feel better to insult someone or argue over that person's ill-informed opinions that you know are wrong in so many ways. If your words could get emotional, ask yourself, "What good could come from a screaming match?" (Cat fights are oh, so unattractive.)

Here's a dilemma: can't stand someone, but you're working together or otherwise related? You may have to reduce some interactions to polite matter-of-fact discussions. Keep your conversations with rude people brief, reserved, inoffensive, and yes, respectful. You don't have to like someone to respect their right to an opinion.

CHAPTER 2

Tailor Your Message

Deciding What to Wear, and Where

Your mouth isn't doing all the work. Your clothes are talking, too! Your outfits may be conducting their own dapper dialogue or a tailoring tragedy.

Planning to go to a prom? A wedding? A soirée of some sort? If you are invited to a formal event, you will want to dress respectfully and appropriately. Your host will give you clues. We know you have individual style and good taste. We also know you want to respect the host's comfort level, so let's review some basic terminology.

Formally speaking . . .

Are you "all tied up" when it comes to formal events? Do you need to review the different requirements of formal wear? Let's review the options.

"White Tie" is the ultimate affair, requiring highly formal evening wear. High-level receptions, ultra-formal affairs, and diplomatic events will call for White Tie. A white vest is worn over a formal shirt with the ultra-formal white bow tie. White gloves are often carried along by the gentleman while dancing. Ladies are expected to wear long, formal evening gowns. Just say "yes" to gloves, gems—the works! This is the occasion when your dress can impress.

The more commonly occurring "Formal" or "Black Tie" event traditionally means tuxedos for the guys and long evening gowns for the ladies. At the present time, many variations on this theme are accepted. Guys have it easy. Rent a tux if you don't have one! Ladies, it's good to go long on the hems, but as styles change, we may have some wiggle room here. It is a good policy to inquire what the hostess will be wearing. We are reminded of how special an occasion is when we must dress up for it.

Of course, as your mother or mentor may have taught you, match those shoes to your bag and your socks with your slacks. Be appropriately dressed from head to toe. There may be a photographer involved; so look camera-ready! Guys, those shoes should shine. Show you know how to pay attention to detail. And there are so many details.

In fashion, nothing's easy. What if "Black Tie Preferred" or "Black Tie Optional" appears on an invitation? Now, what do you wear?

At "Black Tie Preferred" or "Black Tie Optional" occasions, a tuxedo is the preferred male formal attire, although a well-tailored dark suit, white shirt and tie is often accepted. If you go with anything less formal, please be advised . . . it may be considered inappropriate for this type of affair. For the ladies, when the host or hostess says "Optional," you can flaunt your fashion flair in either long or short gowns, or a stylish cocktail dress will work just fine. Consider the effect of your low-cut neckline and revealing hemline. Necklines and hemlines are like temperatures: They can make people uncomfortable when they're too low . . . or too high!

Dimond's Gems

*Necklines
and hemlines
are like temperatures:*

*uncomfortable when
they're too low
or too high!*

When you have any occasion to dress up, take it as an opportunity. Wear something a step above what you would wear everyday. Sometimes just adding the right accessories speaks volumes.

Accessorize, don't dramatize.

According to most dictionary definitions, an accessory is an object not essential in itself. It adds to the beauty, convenience, or effectiveness of something else. Your choice of an accessory is a subordinate, but often significant indication of your nod to good taste.

So do yourself a fashion favor: do an "accessories sweep" before you leap. Sweep by a mirror. Stop and look at yourself. Do your accessories compete with your communicators (your eyes and mouth)? If you want to send an effective message, you might consider removing some of those distractions.

Sweep superfluous ornamentals off your face. For instance, if others are forced to look at your eyebrow ring instead of your eyeballs, you risk losing eye contact. Brow rings may be your ornament of choice for certain occasions, but think about who is looking at that ring before you distract their gaze. Sometimes this type of body ornament is acceptable, yet you may sidetrack others who are intrigued by anything shiny and moving in front of them. They may find your accessory, but lose your message. If you have a piercing near or on your mouth, others may be so intrigued with this gleaming object that they don't actually hear all you have to say. Don't let that little hoop "ring in" all their attention while you are communicating.

Many of us admire creativity and the right to express ourselves. From tattoos to toe rings, let us applaud the accessorized appendage. Yet, remember to apply those accessories with care. Others may fixate on your fabulous fob or your stunning tongue stud. Some may rave about your lip ring or hear the metal clink on your teeth, but did they miss your message?

Again, personal taste is subjective, or as the fashion-conscious French say, "chacun à son goût" (everyone to his or her own taste). Certainly, wear what you feel is comfortable or presents the image you wish to promote. Yet, give yourself a competitive edge and choose your accessories carefully. That involves dressing to meet the demands of the occasion and accessorize with respect. You'll up your chances that others will show the same respect to you.

Sweep the floor . . . the room . . . the venue.

Know where you are going to wear that accessory before you decide to wear it. Who are you going to see? In what activity are you going to partake? For instance, if you are speaking to a large group, you don't want your clothes or accessories to do all the talking. Do you really want attention? You'll get it. But you'll risk being referred to as "that lady with the wild hat" or "that guy with the crazy tie." Ask yourself, "What impression do I want to make?"

"Love that emerald pin! Where did you find it?" That emerald green pin can be your green light. Let the conversation commence! If you are entering a networking situation, an interesting scarf, attractive pin, or unusual handbag can create a great icebreaker. Relationships begin with common bonds. If you feel whimsical, you may wish to wear a pin on your shoulder or sideways. Now, that can be an eye-catcher, so be prepared for the consequences. Someone may be inclined to comment on your creativity . . . or try to help you straighten your jewelry!

Your attire and accessories can truly help you communicate creatively. If you are communicating skillfully, then *you*—not your piercings, pins, or pendants—will be remembered for your message. You don't want your clothing to speak louder than your words.

CHAPTER 3

Dinner Chatter
It's a Mouthful

While we're thinking about good manners, let's dish about dining protocol. Social graces have become subjective. They seem to fluctuate in acceptance like the diet du jour. We must, however, take responsibility for our own manners. You may want to use these delicate directives as a guide before business interviews or dining out with family and friends.

A word for the host: don't be a ghost.

Be visible at all times, from the start to finish of the affair. Welcome your guests and help them become comfortable. Direct them to seating or socializing areas and start the introductions. Once seated, introduce everyone at the table, assisting them with their name on place cards or name tags, whenever possible. Wonder what to do if there are no name tags? Make an effort to use a guest's name each time you address him, and repeat it in conversation.

Identify unusual dishes. Don't leave guests wondering what exactly is in the entrée they're about to enjoy, and be prepared to offer alternate dishes to guests who have allergies or who are on special diets.

Smile! Even in the face of a dining dilemma, your pleasant facial expression makes you appear to be in control. You must set the mood, so try to keep dinner comments on the positive side. Later, when your guests think back and remember their dining experience, they'll be smiling, too.

Be my guest!

All hands on party deck! Dinner affairs often begin with appetizers. That means finger food frenzy. Avoid eating finger foods that are saucy and could require finger licking. Think about it. Was the chicken finger-lickin'? And did you use that hand to shake? Now that's foul.

Don't be a dip at the dip. It's well known that "double dipping" is considered impolite. To avoid the desire to dive back into the dip, just place a handful of crackers or chips on your appetizer plate and apply a dollop of dipping sauce on top.

Claim turf. If you are invited to a numbered table event, scope the room for your row and table. If you have been provided name cards on the table, find your seat and mark it as your own with a ticket or your business card. If you were handed name cards at a reception area, simply place your name card on the plate. You have signaled your presence in case anyone is looking for you. Another benefit: first one to arrive gets the best seat at the table!

Stop, look, and listen. If you are someone's guest, wait to sit until you receive a verbal signal or nonverbal nod to sit down.

My plate or yours? All of us have been faced with this dilemma. Which bread plate belongs to which guest? No worries if there are only two of you facing each other at a small table, but this is a particularly challenging question if you are seated at a table of eight or ten.

To solve this dilemma, just remember this well-known acronym: **BMW**. It's not only a great car, it's great etiquette advice. From left to right it stands for Bread (smaller plate) Meal (larger plate) and Water (glasses). Simple! All smaller plates are on your left, so reach to the left for bread or salad. Sometimes beginning courses are stacked on your main plate.

Dimond's Gems

It can be like playing a game of "diners' dominos."

Now you know the proper plate lineup. One false move and everyone could end up with the wrong plate. Your dinner mates could end up wondering where they should place their warm roll, or they may scurry around for a replacement plate—and this can get ugly. It can be like playing a game of "diners' dominos."

Left is right . . . for lefties. Left-handed people know this rule. Allow them to sit at the left end or at the head of the table. **Listen up!** A similar rule goes for those who are hard of hearing. If someone asks you to switch places, do so without question. There may be a good reason. That person might be able to hear better from one side. Be aware of that fact and respect his or her particular needs.

Less is more. In a restaurant venue, resist any urge to order a more expensive meal than your host. In this case, tact trumps taste buds. Ask your host about his recommendation, then follow that lead. Even if your host is eating salad, he may give you the go-ahead to order more than greens.

If you do the asking, you do the paying. If you are the initiator of the dining date, it's your job to make your guest feel comfortable. And if you feel generous, be sure to point out the possibilities on the menu. You might say, "I hear the filet mignon is fabulous. I hope you are hungry!" This allows your guest to feel you aren't limiting him or her to what you are ordering, even if you are eating light.

It's neat to be neat. Avoid messy food, from soup to dessert. Order food that can be eaten with a knife and fork. Finger foods can be messy. Exceptions are informal dining, light snacking, and cultural or ethnic protocol.

Little dabs will do ya. Be kind to your napkin. It is meant to be dabbed at your lips. Simply unfold it and place it on your lap. If your napkin drops on the floor and is unreachable, do not attempt a circus move to retrieve it. Politely request a new one.

Most importantly, do not mistake the napkin for a tissue. If you do need a tissue, step away from the dining area and dispose of the tissue before returning to your seat.

No elbows, Mac! Even kids know this one: keep those elbows off the table. Sure, you can lean forward just a bit. That shows you are interested in the conversation. But avoid "elbowing" your way in to conversations, tables, or just about anything in polite society.

Now serving! You must wait until everyone at the table has been seated and served to start your meal, unless your host insists that you begin. (There may be a delay in serving everyone in a timely manner.)

Halt before you salt. Don't insult the chef. Avoid seasoning your food before you have even tasted it.

Don't play table Twister®. Resist the urge to reach over your dining partner to grab your seasoning of choice. Simply ask for the salt or pepper to be passed to you. If you are extremely fortunate, your host has provided mini salt and pepper shakers at your setting, thus allowing you to avoid that nasty reach.

If someone requests salt from across the table, simply pick up both shakers. They should be passed person to person around the table. In formal occasions, don't intercept someone's salt pass by taking a quick hit on your food.

What to do when your fork runs away with your spoon. Lost in utensil madness? Just remember to work from the outside toward your plate. Start with the outermost utensils and gradually use each fork, knife, and spoon.

Quite Continental. How you hold your utensils is up to you and your comfort level. Using Continental style, the fork stays in your left hand, tines down. The knife stays in your right hand. Your knife may be used to cut, slide, and secure the food on your fork. There's no need to switch the fork to the right hand. The cut food is transferred on the down-facing fork directly to your mouth with your left hand. Many Europeans accept this practice and it has become more and more popular in the United States.

Hold everything! If you are a fan of the North American style, it is common to use a fork, held like a pencil in your right hand. To cut food, you may wish to simply take your fork in your left hand and turn the tines down. The knife is taken in the right hand. Cut with that knife, then rest it on the edge of the plate with the blade facing inward. Then, switch your fork to the right hand, stab the food and carry it to your mouth. Some choose to turn the tines up. If you are left-handed, you may reverse the process. Sound complicated? Not really. As long as you are using your fork, not your fingers, you do not need to stress about making a mess.

Rules for the "Knives of the Round Table." In many dining experiences, it is not considered polite to let your dirty knife, fork, or spoon touch the table. Soup bowls, shrimp cocktail cups, and teacups are usually presented with a plate underneath. During dinner, use those plates on which to set your used flatware.

Seeking second servings? Place the knife and fork on the right side of the plate, leaving some room for the food.

Requesting a temporary leave of absence? If you must leave the table momentarily, be sure to cross your knife with your fork, tines down, in a "V" shape, with the open space of the "V" facing you. It's a well-known signal to your server, saying, "I am only resting, not finished yet."

When you have completed a course, let your utensils give the "Stop" signal. Simply line up your knife and fork diagonally on the plate. Your server will know that course may be removed.

Chew before chatter. Of course, this is a standard. Please do not chew with your mouth open. It's so unattractive!

Soup's on! Spoon's away! Always move the soup spoon away from your body and fill it up two-thirds of its capacity. Then, sip the liquid sideways without inserting the whole bowl of the spoon in the mouth. Slurping is probably the worst thing someone can do when eating soup. It is appropriate to tilt the bowl away from the body to get the last spoonful or two.

Dessert dilemma. Your mouth is watering. You've managed to reward yourself and have saved room for dessert. But what do you use to eat that "Death by Chocolate"? Look at the top of your plate. Ah, there your dessert utensils are, placed horizontally on the table, near the top of your plate. No dessert utensils? Just wait and you shall receive. They are usually brought to the table with the dessert.

Don't dip the dessert spoon into the coffee. When coffee and tea are served, an appropriate, delicate teaspoon will be provided. Don't be an alien to this rule: use your saucer.

Curb your doggie bag. It is improper to ask for a take-home bag when you are a guest. An exception would be if your host insists. Then you can take that puppy home.

Serve light conversation. Keep that dinner conversation lighthearted. Controversial subjects such as religion, sex, or politics can be bad for digestion.

Mixed drinks and mixed signals. Is your host serving wine or liquor? If you enjoy an alcoholic beverage, do so in moderation. Avoid any chance of losing control of your conversation, particularly in business settings. Remember the saying, "An intoxicated person's words are a sober person's thoughts."

No one's perfect. Are you angst-ridden about using the wrong fork or spoon? Are you still alive to tell about it? Relax and get over it. Please, enjoy dining as a delightful combination of conversation and food consumption. If you are confident and perhaps a little self-deprecating, your associates will not admonish your mishaps and you will be remembered fondly.

CHAPTER 4

Phone Manners Matter
Don't Be a Ringy Dingy!

Are you aware of the benefits of telephone etiquette?

Y ou will find it's valuable to take time to mind your phone manners, from the first impression at an office reception desk or professional conference call to personal discussions with friends and family.

Be aware. Listen to the sound of your own voice. You can set the mood of the call. Your phone power will increase if you are aware of how others hear your voice and inflection. What is your voice's attitude? You may be surprised that if you are upbeat, often your phone partner's voice will reflect that positive attitude, too.

Be polite. Good manners are essential for pleasant conversations. Your polite phone protocol will set the mood and increase your chances of positive responses. For instance, instead of demanding, "What's your name?" respectfully ask, "May I please have your name?" After you receive his or her name, use it in conversation. For difficult conversations, remain pleasant, or at least calm and in control.

Be helpful. "How may I help you?" Incoming calls should not be treated as nuisances. They may be requests for assistance or information. Being helpful requires patience, empathy, and concern for the callers' needs. Share information to lead them in the right direction.

Be concerned. Discover what your phone partners need. Show that you care about what happens to their calls and that you value their time. Instead of saying, "We can't do that," a better option may be, "Let me check. I'll find out what we can do for you." You may decide simply to provide a caller with an alternative name, contact, or number to lead him or her in the right direction.

Be consistent and you'll be your best. You'll increase your chances of better phone relations by showing you want to solve your callers' problems, questions, or concerns. They will remember you for your consistently positive attitude, your concern, helpfulness, and your attention to their needs.

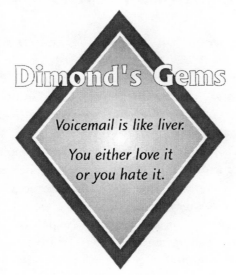

Dimond's Gems

Voicemail is like liver.

You either love it or you hate it.

Va va va voicemail.

"We're not available to take your call right now . . ."

Voicemail is a lot like liver. You either love it or you hate it. Either way, it has become part of our culture. Since we are a society compelled to leave phone messages, be sure you leave a good one. Take those opportunities to practice your voicemail delivery skills.

Whether you're giving or receiving voicemail, ask yourself, are you missing valuable information due to poorly worded messages? Are you rambling, getting tongue-tied, tripped-up or becoming (duh) instantly inarticulate when you record? Are you cringing when listening to long, drawn-out messages that are left for you to decipher?

Not to worry. Like many communication skills, it takes a bit of practice and playback before we're truly effective on voicemail.

Ring, ring! You've reached a record-ing!

Reduce phone message misery by applying these tips.

Prepare to call collect-ed. Collect your thoughts. Be composed when you call. You'll be easier to understand if you speak thoughtfully. Try not to make up your message as you go along.

Plan your talking points, even if you must jot them down. This is particularly helpful if you must make an appointment or a business call. You'll be less likely to go off on a tangent before the dreaded beep cuts you off.

Make it snappy! Record your message within a minute. A good voicemail is a quick voicemail. Be sure to get the following info into your message:

1. Your name. If you are not a frequent caller to this number, spell it so the listener can understand it.
2. Your contact number. Provide an area code for out-of-town calls.
3. Your message. Don't simply leave your name and number. Be sure to say what you want, need, or desire.
4. Your contact info one more time. Repeat your name and number before saying goodbye.

The art of articulation. Huh? What did she say? Was it "*stay in the car*" or "*sympathy card*"? Some phrases can sound alike. Practice the art of speaking clearly and succinctly to increase your chances of getting your point across. Say your phone number clearly, not in a rush at the end of your sentence, and give the recipient time to write your info down.

How to kill a message. Beep! Silence . . ."Oh yes, one more thing. Congratulations! You've won the million dollar sweepstakes and must return this call today to be eligible to collect your prize. Am I still recording? Hello?"

It's tempting to try to pack a lot of info in one short message, but hit your headlines and highlights right away. Give the caller enough information to be useful. A lengthy, complicated message can be deadly on voicemail, especially if you are calling a busy person or someone with a lot of messages to answer while traveling. If your voicemail is too detailed or strung together, the listener may even cut it off halfway through, so please, don't save your best for last.

Now introducing . . . the complex message. Some complicated messages are simply beyond voicemail. Detailed messages should be politely introduced, not outlined and analyzed. If your message is simply too multifaceted for voicemail, be sure to ask for some time to talk in real time or in person.

Mixed messages. If you have two or more messages, state that clearly at the beginning so the listener is prepared to hear all of your points. A good rule is to say, "I have two messages to give you. The first is . . . ."

Voicemail is powerful. Use with care. When at all possible, avoid leaving upsetting, emotional or extremely bad news by voicemail. If it is essential to get in touch with you immediately, say so on your message. Clearly state your contact information. If there is another number you would like to share or if you wish to be paged or taken out of a meeting when the person returns your call, tell the recipient how to find you. Then try to be available for the call. If possible, try to arrange to see him or her to deliver the message in real time, face to face.

Review your outgoing message.

What do your callers hear? We have already focused on the importance of leaving an effective voice message. Now it is essential to provide your callers with a clear, polite, positive outgoing message so they know who they've reached.

Since this is personal, you must be comfortable with your outgoing message. You may want to get creative. If you are not creative, however, leave a basic message with "just the facts ma'am." You may wish to leave your name and number or just a number with no name. You may wish to say, "*We* are not available . . ." instead of "*I* am not available . . ." Write a few lines and read them aloud. Record your message and play it back. Do you like it? Are you comfortable?

Your message is a reflection of you. You may even want to call your own number from another phone and listen to it. Ask yourself if you provide enough information to the incoming caller, if you are comfortable with your inflection and attitude, and if the message sounds like you. If you are not comfortable with your outgoing message, re-record it. If you are still having trouble, simply ask someone you trust to record it for you.

And . . . you're *out*! Use your outgoing message when you are out-going. If you are going to be away from your office for vacation, it's a good idea to record an extended absence greeting on your voicemail. It's a great way to let callers know you will not be available to return calls until a later date.

If there is someone who can take your calls or if there are other numbers that would be useful to your callers, you can provide them in your message. If you are traveling for business reasons, but still checking messages, be sure to indicate that information on your outgoing message.

The great message makeover.

Nobody's perfect, so most do not need to strive for voicemail perfection. If just one of these tips improves your voicemail-ability, we're on the right track.

If you find yourself saying, "I don't believe I said that!" after you leave a voice message, it's time to review your skills.

Sometimes it's too late before we realize we'd like to have a do-over. Thankfully, some voicemail systems let you playback, review, and (this is the best part) even re-record your message. This is a wonderful option for those who may gamble with a ramble or who just hate to say goodbye.

Finally, remember that voicemail can be a powerful tool, yet we still can't beat good old-fashioned conversation for valuable emotions, expressions, and the human touch. Use your voicemail as a tool, not a crutch.

CHAPTER 5

Applaud, Admire, and Appreciate
Adopting an Aptitude
for Gratitude and Graciousness

When was the last time you composed a handwritten thank you note? Remember, a simple thank you contributes to the foundation of good relationships. It makes the recipient feel great. In these days of technology, we even welcome the sight of emailed thank you notes.

Think of the feelings you experienced the last time you received a handwritten thank you in the mail. Share that feeling. Refresh your thank you note know-how.

Remember to say "thanks."

Say "thanks" early and often. Of course, good etiquette states that there are the classic and formal times to express your thanks, for instance, after a birthday, holiday, wedding, or promotion. Other occasions include baby showers, hospitality, fundraising, job interviews, volunteerism, and expressions of sympathy. But here are four occasions you may not have considered. They involve personal support, favors, encouragement, and loyalty.

1. Has someone told you they care about you? Do you have a friend or colleague who occasionally "checks in" with you just to see if you're okay? Is there a family member who is always there for you when you need him or her? These are the people in our lives who deserve a heartfelt, handwritten thank you note, and so much more. Take a moment to compose a few lines such as, "I want you to know how much I appreciate you." Then give a recent example of the gesture of kindness.

2. Has someone gone above and beyond for you? Has someone filled-in for you in a meeting or an event when you couldn't be there yourself? Has a neighbor done a favor lately? Has your co-worker completed a project ahead of time? If so, a personal thank you will make his or her day. "I know I can always count on you!" are great words with which to begin your note.

3. Has someone encouraged you or given you a pep talk? Sometimes we need to hear from others to remind us of our abilities and our strengths. Take a moment and jot down a few lines simply to let that person know, "You are my inspiration."

4. Has someone spoken highly of you? Did someone recently recommend you as a great choice for a social committee or professional position? Has one of your colleagues included a few promotional words or a verbal "ad" for you in conversation with friends? Since your good reputation depends on word of mouth, this is a perfect time to let that person know how much you appreciate the kind words. You can begin your expression of gratitude with, "Thank you for your kind words." If it's a professional recommendation, you may suggest you are honored by the gesture.

A few words can go a long way.

When sending thank you notes, your words should be handwritten, if possible. After all, how often do we have the chance to see handwriting in the age of email and voicemail? Your notes' recipients will appreciate knowing you put pen to paper and actually composed a note just for them.

Dimond's Gems

Did it make you smile or sigh?

Then send a thank you in reply.

Your selection of words should reveal your true appreciation for the gift or kind act. It's easy. Just think of what you'd like to see in a thank you note if it were addressed to you. Did it make you smile or sigh? Then send a thank you in reply.

Note necessities.

Some of us consider these short notes a special challenge. Here are my suggestions for what should be mentioned in a thank you note.

Remember your purpose. Be sure to say "thank you" or another expression of appreciation, gratitude, admiration, or respect somewhere in your note. Be sure to state the name of the gift, gesture, or act. Express your thoughts with enthusiasm in your own words. Even though others can give you guidelines, your note should sound like you.

Expand your message. Let the recipient know how you intend to use that gift, how much you value the experience, or how you may invest the gift money*. For example, "We cherish your thoughtful wedding gift. We will think of you each time we fill our crystal vase with fresh flowers," or "We smile each time we remember the delightful dinner at your lovely home. We appreciate your hospitality more than this simple card can say," or "Thank you for making the trip to Pennsylvania to attend my graduation. I will always treasure the photo of you standing beside me at Old Main." Another example would be, "Please accept my sincere thanks for your generous graduation gift. I intend to use it toward purchasing my new computer."

*Research shows there are those who recommend mentioning the dollar amount involved in a gift of money. Others recommend simply writing a grateful statement directed toward the giver's generosity, thoughtfulness, or extravagance with no mention of a dollar amount. It's up to you.

Make the recipient(s) feel special. Express your personal, sincere appreciation. Let your thank you card recipients know you care about their investment of money, time, or thoughtfulness.

Note no-no's.

Prevent the paper pile up. Don't let your thank you notes get stale. Write while your feelings are fresh. If you wait too long to reply, you may lose your enthusiasm. To regain lost energy, think about the person or people who gave you their time, talent, or a treasure while you're writing. Of course, there are etiquette timelines for almost every occasion, but the best rule is, "the earlier the better." Your note will be well-received if it is written at your earliest convenience.

"Thank you," however, has no expiration date. Your note will be appreciated whenever it is received. In this busy day and age, people quite understand about time constraints, demanding schedules, and delays. Yet, we always appreciate when someone goes beyond our expectations and sends a prompt pronouncement of appreciation.

Avoid the "all about me" syndrome. Avoid the use of the word "I" when you have to include your other half. Give your husband, wife, or significant other a name if you are writing for two. If you are writing on behalf of a family or an entire group, mention them in your thank you note. "John and I wish to thank you . . ." or "My sister Jane, my brother Jim, and I wish to thank you . . ." or "The College Choir joins me in thanking you . . ." are good examples.

Don't drop anyone. So, you didn't like the gift? It's certain to happen. Even if your taste or expectations may not match the gift, avoid words that express the least hint of your disinterest or disappointment. A gift is a kindness. Kindnesses are rare. Be grateful and be gracious.

Don't generalize; personalize. If you receive a gift from a couple or a family, you may write one note to both or all, with each of the names given on the gift card written in.

If you receive a present from a formal group or club, you may send the entire group a thank you note. Simply make it clear you wish all of them to see it. Be sure you ask for it to be posted or circulated to reach everyone. They will be glad you acknowledged their individual contributions and they'll appreciate the time you took to thank them.

Note negotiables.

Handwritten cards can be keepsakes. Yet, if you cannot find the time to write a note, do express your feelings otherwise, such as by phone or email. A sincere thank you is always appreciated.

When in doubt, send it out!

Gentle gestures are so rare. That's why people delight in receiving your occasional expressive note, email, or call of thanks for anything, on any day.

Your friends, colleagues, and associates will appreciate the gracefulness and good taste of your personalized thank you. No matter how well it's written, most recipients will agree; your heartfelt message is the key. Thoughtfulness travels. A few kind words or lines can go a long way.

PART TWO

Pitch Like a Pro!
From Job Interviews
to Social Schmooze

CHAPTER 6

Gotta Getta Job?
Getta Clue

The dream: You've pitched yourself into the job of a lifetime.

The reality: A great career usually begins with an investment of time, work, and energy. With a little knowledge and a lot of chutzpah, you can put some finesse into your appearance and approach. Up your chances of getting the job you want or need to improve your life and lifestyle. Guide yourself to the good life with a close look at how you pitch and present yourself.

Knowledge is power. How many times have you heard that? It has never been more true than when applying for a job. If you want to uncover new opportunities, be prepared to do some digging. Find out details on the key skill sets, training, or experience the employer will be looking for in you, the job candidate. What's the company's mission statement? How do they describe themselves in brochures, pamphlets, or on the Internet? If you can, review a copy of their annual report. Your research will help you tailor your resume and the interview to "wow" your potential employer.

Talk the talk. Become an ideal job candidate by putting some custom-tailored effort into your search. Mirror the employer's language based on the written description in the job ad, the tone used on the company's Web site, and collateral material. Tell them who you are and why you want the job in their own terms. Repeat some corporate phrasing in your cover letter, which of course, is the introductory letter you'll use to complement your best sales piece—your resume.

Write your cover letter with language that suits the occasion. For instance, you may write about your "competencies," but you know you are simply listing your skills. Respect the language the employer uses. If the language is formal, be formal. If it's more relaxed, be more relaxed. Ask for the job in the company's own jargon.

Avoid these four-letter words: "just" and "only." These little words can poison your presentation. If you say, "I'm *only* interested in *just* a part time position," or "I'm *only* looking here for the benefits," or "I *just* have a . . . degree," those four-letter phrases *just* may have underwhelmed the interviewer. You could have eroded your effectiveness with those power-sucking sentences. Stop using those four-letter words in public! When in doubt, cut 'em out.

Write your resume like an ad. Yeah, yeah. You've heard it far too often: employers get thousands of resumes each year. It's a safe bet that your resume will be quickly skimmed, not really deciphered; so write it like an ad. As in any advertisement, your best features should be highlighted up front. Show that you are not only interested in the job, you are an interesting person. Your words need to be visually inviting.

It takes work to compose a killer resume. Find out what works. Review samples of resumes that your friends used to land their jobs. Check the Internet for samples of resumes. Then individualize your masterpiece. Your resume should tell more than who you are; it should highlight what you know. That's essential before you launch headfirst into the interview process. Target your goal and briefly state it. Your cover letter and resume are your best advertisements before you walk into a room or speak your first words. And be sure to give your professional references a heads-up that you're conducting an active job search so they can prepare to talk you up.

Tweak your 'tude. Assuming the potential employer has a short attention span (yes, assume this), you must convince him or her with your resume and cover letter that you are the solution to their search for the perfect employee. Don't think the company, organization, or group is the answer to your job needs. Not at all. You are in control. Actually, you are the answer to the company's hiring needs. If you change your attitude, you will change your entire approach to landing the job. Make it an easy choice to select you above all other candidates. Be confident, not cocky. You must tell how your particular skills will be a great asset to the company and that you'd be honored to join this excellent organization. If you give positive energy, you'll get positive energy. Be respectful and you'll be respected.

A good resume will simply get you in the door. After all that written preparation, you'll still need to sell yourself in person.

Present a nice package. Congratulations. They read your ad (resume) and your promotional piece (cover letter). They like you. They really like you! You are called in for the interview. There you are, ready to take the first steps into an office for your interview. So how do you complete your winning package?

Believe it or not, admit it or not, perception is reality. If you look confident, you will be more confident. Most of the time, this theory works. You may have heard that failing to prepare means you're preparing to fail.

Dimond's Gems

*Don't explain
that your long-term goal
is to replace the
interviewer.*

Get ready. Before the interview date, select what you'll want to wear. This sounds like a given, but it can be a deal-breaker. If you must travel to interview, be sure to double-check your suitcase. Do you have everything? We don't know why, but many candidates say they often forget to pack appropriate shoes! From head to toe, be sure to dress suitably. It takes only a few minutes to establish the company's fashion frame of mind. Call the receptionist or assistant ahead to inquire about the dress code, if any. Discover these dapper details: Does this company recognize Casual Friday? Or is the Chairman of the Board visiting the office on the interview date? In this first interview, try to go a bit more conservative. Be sure you highlight your skills, not your skirt or shirt. You'll be glad you did.

Practice your interview presentation in front of a mirror or with a friend. If possible, videotape your simulated interview. With practice, you will be able to get a good idea of how the interviewer will see you. Check your words and your inflection (verbals) as well as your body language (nonverbals). Do you look and sound like a great candidate who radiates confidence?

Get set. Bring two copies of your resume so you can follow along with the employer during your interview. Arrive early, prepared for relationship-building. Acknowledge that you know you're early and you'll gladly wait your opportunity to be received and reviewed.

The beginning of the interview is the classic get-to-know-you time. Walk in, not only with confidence, but with real respect for the other people's schedules. Know the name of your interviewer. Be careful to pronounce his or her name correctly. Respect each person you meet as you arrive at the office. Be patient and polite, even if you had to wait longer than expected for your interview.

Go! Your time in a job interview usually flies by quickly and you may not recall much of what you said. To make the most of your short time and "sell yourself," think of this as a rare and wonderful opportunity for this Don't/Do exercise.

Don't assume you know all there is to know about the company or the interviewer's needs.

Don't wait until the last minute to get directions to the interview.

Don't arrive late for an interview or without sufficient time to freshen up and look your best.

Don't underestimate the receptionist or the executive assistant. That person holds access to the interviewer for follow-up and phone calls.

Don't forget your manners or lose your cool, even if you are disappointed with the way the interview is going.

Don't place blame on any person or situation when speaking of intolerable past jobs or supervisors.

Don't say you want this job just to make ends meet between other gigs.

Don't test your interviewer's tolerance for tattoos. (Don't let your tattoo do the talking!)

Don't explain that your long-term goal is to replace the interviewer.

Do have a handy list of talking points. (What do they need to know about you?)

Do learn to bridge back to your talking points and play to your strengths during the interview.

Do participate with enthusiasm and positive energy.

Do ask questions of the interviewer to show you are interested in details of the business or organization.

Do feel well rehearsed and ready, thanks to your practice sessions with colleagues or your rehearsal on video camera.

Do respect everyone you meet throughout the course of the interview, from the security desk to CEO suite!

Do continue to seek training and refresher courses to conquer your interviewing fears. Keep up with the latest information in your field. This education may eventually qualify you for a higher income.

Do keep your sense of humor. No one is perfect, so if you drip coffee on your jacket, simply laugh and say it's a "*designer*" suit and now *everyone* will want one!

A bonus **Do** for you: If you are more *interested*, you may even become more *interesting!*

Follow up and chill out. It's not over yet. Review the business cards you've collected. We know the value of a heartfelt thank you note. Immediately send a personal, handwritten thank you note to all involved in your interview process. Good follow-up is the most effective way to turn your interview into a job. Be sure to mention your enthusiasm about joining that company or organization.

Now *that's* an attractive way to start a new career.

CHAPTER 7

The Pitcher's Negotiation Dilemma
Spell Negotiation with 3 R's:
Respect, Reflect, Redirect!

It's a fact of life and sometimes a key to survival: no matter who you are or what you do, everyone must negotiate. You negotiate whether you're at work, at home, at the market, or at the mall. You bargain with your kids, your colleagues, and your clients. You can negotiate the car pool schedule, a business contract, a vacation, a new car, a promotion, or a new relationship.

Negotiation "steamrollers" leave the other party feeling flat.

You might think with all that negotiation practice you're getting, you'd be great at it. The truth is, you may not know how good you are until you take a closer look at yourself.

If you come into a negotiation as a steamroller, you'll leave the other party feeling flat. Instead, make them feel they have actually benefited from the experience of working with you toward alternatives and solutions. Negotiation is about partnering with people, not pounding them into the ground.

If you want more success in your negotiations, you'll need a plan and an informed approach.

Consider adding these **R**'s to your next negotiation:

Respect: Respect can be spelled with another "**R**"—Research. Identify and discover each party's potential benefits and personal or professional interests. Ask yourself, "What's the party's motivation? What would make them comfortable? Reasonably happy? Ecstatic?" We know it takes two to tango! Take yourself out of your position and do the negotiation dance in their shoes.

Reflect: Present your side of the negotiation in words the other party can appreciate. Reflect or mirror their mood and style. If you must be more formal to negotiate with this party, then assume that formal approach. If the other party is more casual, be more casual. Look closely and find the options that are available.

Redirect: Yet another "**R**" plays a great role in this step. This takes just a bit of finesse, but after respecting another's opinion and reflecting their needs, you can move the negotiation to your side of the table with confidence. You will present a better case if you exude poise and certainty.

How do you know you're negotiating properly? It has been argued that there is no best way to negotiate; so you must do what works for you. No matter how you get to a negotiated agreement, you must persuade the other party that your settlement has fulfilled a need, provided a creative solution, or brought a benefit. If you are satisfied at the end of the negotiation, then you did it well.

Here are seven simple starter strategies to help you get ahead. If you apply these tips at the start of the negotiation process, you may find yourself closer to negotiation success.

1. **Identify your strengths before you negotiate.** You are probably stronger than you think. Do your homework. Prepare to say who you are or whom you represent. State what you want to accomplish and why you wish to accomplish it.

2. **Believe in yourself.** Show you know that the deal you're offering is the best available. Your self-confidence will help you gain respect from those on the other side. Be clear about your objectives and show the satisfying benefits of reaching an agreement.

3. **Know who's in the negotiation with you.** Know and respect the authority of each person in the room. Do not underestimate anyone. For instance, you must know whether you're negotiating with the decision maker or a representative.

4. **Listen to what others are saying.** Gather vital information to increase mutual understanding. Reflect and repeat what you hear. Show respect through your listening skills. This increases your goodwill and can ultimately influence a positive outcome.

5. **Avoid inflexible bottom-line thinking.** Reach a fair agreement without giving away too much, but don't limit the options at the start. Remember, others need to gain or benefit from dealing with you. Show you've done your research to clarify the interests of both sides.

6. **Get off the emotional rollercoaster.** Anger can become a tactic in negotiation. Sometimes the person displaying the anger is trying to show seriousness or simply wants to intimidate. It may be tempting, but do not counteract the other side's anger with your anger. When you encounter intimidation tactics, take a moment and simply address the problem at hand. Refocus. Be firm, yet fair. Re-establish everyone's commitment to a mutually beneficial outcome.

Be calm and confident. You'll be heard as the "voice of reason" at the negotiation table.

7. **What is your "take home settlement?"** It's probably somewhere between your best case and your worst case scenario. It's your "settlement scope." You've really won if you can reach a consensus within your settlement scope. Be aware of your bottom line. If your settlement falls below that line, you won't like the deal. You could risk losing your initiative or you might become less interested in following through with your end of the bargain.

Now that you have your starter list, look ahead. Think about how the outcome of your negotiations might affect your future relationships. Ensure your potential for future dealings by looking at the big picture. Focus on issues, not personalities. We are often remembered more for our approach than anything else. It's not always whether we've won every negotiation that makes us a winner, but how we've conducted ourselves along the way.

Remember, respect the needs of others along with your own, and voilà! You'll have a successful negotiation, not a confrontation.

CHAPTER 8

Your Personal Sales Pitch
Networking Is Not All About You

Want to pitch yourself without striking out? Take the focus off of you and you'll take the *work* out of net*work*ing!

Caution: Too much "wind" in your personal sales pitch can blow away your chances of being heard or understood. Self-marketing is a skill that is essential for effective communications and fabulous first impressions. Whether you're on or off the job, you can sell your skills and services to others every day. The key is to stay focused on others' needs.

Give 'em schmooze they can use!

May I help you? Colleagues, contacts, and potential clients should feel comfortable coming to you when they have a particular need, issue, or challenge. They'll want to know what you can do for them. So be ready to tell them. Be prepared to let others know exactly who you are and what you are capable of doing without overselling yourself.

Don't blow smoke into your speech.

Filter your foggy words and you will clear up your message. Although you may hear and use certain words, phrasing, or jargon every day, do not assume that others know or understand your terminology. You can build trust and define your message by speaking the language of those listening to you. Adjust your approach to meet their needs. If you talk in words the public can understand, you can make your points with ease. Casual gatherings call for a casual approach. Public speaking presentations and job interviews require a respectfully formal technique.

Carefully choose your words. Use speech patterns that make others feel comfortable. This shows you respect their needs. Avoid the urge to impress with improvisation. Be specific about what you can deliver. You don't need to blow smoke to send your signals.

Wipe out that gobbledygook.

Make your message short and simple. If you have a complicated message, pare it down to size. A little trimming can clarify the meaning of your presentation. Smaller bites are often easier to digest.

Cut the qualifiers. If something is important to know, there's no need to say, "It's really, really soooooooooo very important to know . . ." Try saying, "It's crucial to know . . ." or "It's essential to know . . ." Such phrases give a concise meaning to your statement.

Hack down those hedges. As we said in Chapter 6, don't hide behind unnecessary four-letter hedges, such as "just" or "only." When introducing yourself, pump up your presentation power by eliminating the use of "just" and "only" in front of your name. You must admit, "Hi, it's just Jane . . ." and "Hi, it's only Jane . . ." are not as commanding or self-assured as "Hi, it's Jane!" Now, you're talkin'. When in doubt, simply cut the hedges out.

Breeze into others' styles. If you are involved in a casual conversation, your rapping rules can bend with the wind. If you know your acquaintance enjoys a little lighthearted banter, you can be effective if you cater to their affection or wordplay. It puts the fun in the *fun*damentals of discussion.

Speak in a comfortable tone. Naturally, your speaking style will alter depending upon whether you're addressing a professional group or a business colleague. Your style will alter even more if you are speaking with a friend or a best friend. Fine-tune or completely change your style to meet their needs.

Be your own best salesperson. Marketing yourself is as easy as 1, 2, 3. Be concise. It's the "FAB" secret salespeople know. Think of three of your best Features, Advantages, or Benefits. What do you want others to know about you or your company? Write those three items on a cheat sheet and remember to weave them into your next presentation.

Windbreaker: the powerful pause. You can eliminate those windy "umms" and "uhhs" by inserting short breaks to catch the air in your speech. When you have the urge to say "umm," simply stop for a moment and regroup. Pause, then continue. This takes—uh—practice, but it's—umm—going to improve the way others hear your personal sales pitch. Rehearse your introduction or marketing message on audiotape. Count how many times you say the "umm" or "uh" sounds. Try recording your message again until you can do it without the added sound effects.

Now it's time to put your new self-marketing skills to work.

Work the room fearlessly. Yes, even if you are scared stiff.

Name two of our biggest fears . . .

◊   Public presentations
◊   Meeting new people

What is networking?
Combine both of those fears, and there you have it.

Be a GEM:
Generous, Energetic
and Memorable!

The facets of being a GEM at networking:

New business contacts and influential friends meet every day in networking situations. Yet, some of us dread the thought of facing a crowd of new faces. You might ask, "Why do I have to do this? I know enough people already!" Positive rapport is essential for the future of most businesses. It could depend on your ability to work a room. Be a **GEM**. Generous, Energetic, and Memorable!

Yes! Bring your business cards. Of course, you'll want to make connections that will last after the event. But don't rely on those cards to speak for you. It's up to you to move into the crowd and strike up a conversation. And here's a hint: bring a mint!

No! Don't run into a hospitality room just to build your deck of business cards, munch on mini-quiches, open (or close) the bar, and leave. Be generous with your time and talk. Good networking is rooted in relationships.

Take the focus off of you. People are interesting. Be truly interested in others. Avoid the I, me, and mine syndrome. You won't relate to others if you go on talking about how interesting *you* are. You will relate to others when you focus on how interesting *they* are. Practice the art of paying attention. Don't be frenetic. Be energetic!

"Who are you and why are you here?" When you are asked the ultimate question, "What do you do?" have an engaging, specific answer that will stay in their memory. Try to add something relevant and lighthearted in your answer. Don't take yourself too seriously in an initial networking situation. Most people can gather a lot of information about your importance from the title or position listed on your business card. You don't have to remind them of your rank, status, or significance. If you are memorable, others will think about you and enjoy contacting you after the networking session.

Think small. Good comprehensive networking consists of many mini-conversations. You might call it small talk, but there's nothing "small" about it! Small talk discloses interesting facts about you and what you think is humorous, engaging, or important. Small talk can create a common, comfortable bond in your general discussion. This initial short one-to-one conversation can help to put others at ease.

What's safe for small talk? Simply look around you to find comfortable topics to add to your conversation, such as good food, a lovely venue, the function's good cause, or your great host. Keep it positive. No need to recount the details of the case of hives you suffered as a result of your mushroom allergy. We don't need that visual at the veggie tray!

Avoid awkward topics, such as sex, religion, and politics. You'll be sorry you stepped in that conversation quicksand. The deeper you get into those subjects, the harder it'll be to get out.

Develop conversation courage. Do you play it safe and mix only with your business colleagues and good friends when you're in a crowd? Why stick together? Divide and conquer the room! Regroup later and compare notes. You might be surprised what you're missing if you don't venture into the group and communicate with others. Learn how to mingle in and out of conversations, while respecting others' comfort level and space. Start with achievable objectives. Tell yourself you'll meet three new people. Then, do it!

Ask for directions. "May I join you?" Body language can be a guide to working the room. Learn to approach those who exhibit "open" body language. How can you tell? They may be standing alone, facing toward you or they may have a pleasant expression on their face.

People who stand face-to-face (not making eye contact with you) are exhibiting "closed" body language. How can you tell when it's a "closed" conversation? Their nonverbal signals are meant for each other, not the room. It would be a challenge for anyone new to enter their space and exchange a few words. You'd have to force yourself to be noticed. You don't want to have to tap-tap-tap someone on the shoulder to get their attention, unless they're expecting you or, of course, if it's an emergency! Closed body language often indicates people are engaged in an ongoing conversation. If they stop talking and start looking around the room, others may be welcome to join them. This takes some practice, but you can do it!

Blow a verbal kiss. Give compliments and communicate with kind words. Be sure you don't overlook or underestimate anyone. Be gracious to all in the room. Be grateful for the valuable time others spend with you. You may receive a kind word in return. That's worth the effort!

"Bye-Bye! Call me! Don't forget to write!" Before you take off, jot down something you discussed on the back of the other person's business card or write a note to yourself about something memorable you discussed in your "small talk." Be sure to follow up with a call or an email if you promised to do so. Do not make promises or offers you cannot keep after your networking event. People have long memories if they are given false assurances during casual banter.

Escape the name drain.

"And you are . . . . ?" It's happened to all of us—the nasty "name drain." It's when you can see someone important or famous in your mind's eye, but you just can't say his or her name. How embarrassing. If you simply cannot come up with a name, it can turn a friendly introduction into an instantly awkward moment.

For the most part, we can say this name memory loss is

completely understandable and forgivable, since it is so common. Others can empathize with you. It's usually temporary. It's likely you'll remember the name after you relax, and often, when it's too late or inconvenient, like when you're watching TV or when you're in the shower. The question is: can you benefit by remembering names? Of course, you can.

Name your advantage. Everyone can become more effective by remembering names. This is a valuable life communication skill. Whether you're the president of a major corporation, a volunteer in an organization or fundraiser, a student or teacher, name recollection can give you a professional and social advantage.

There's a right way to tag your name—that's right. When applying a name tag, many people choose to do the "Pledge of Allegiance" hand-over-the-heart approach. Right-handers often pick up and apply that tag on the left side by slapping the tag from their right hand onto the left lapel. Some people get more creative and wear their name tags on their handbags or even on their belts. That can create an identity dilemma. Why? Because others need to be able to see your name and you should respect their need to know your identity.

Here's a solution to assist you: Take the focus off of your needs and think about what the person standing in front of you sees as they are trying to remember your name. Don't make them hunt for your name on your left lapel (shifting their eyes) or worse yet, search around your waist for your name. That could be a bit embarrassing!

Instead, try this approach to name tags: Ask a friend to pretend he or she doesn't know your name. Apply your name tag on your right lapel. Extend your right hand to shake hands. Now, ask your friend to shake your hand while searching for your name. Discover how easy it is for your friend to see your name as his gaze glides up your arm to your name tag, then to your eyes. Your name tag can give your colleagues the info they need along the way. No awkward searching for names necessary!

Name tag trends and tips: You may try to get a name tag that can be displayed in a plastic casing attached to a chain or cord around your neck. This name tag necklace is a good choice if you wish to protect your best suit. Yet, be cautious about the angle of the dangle. Sometimes those name tags can twist and turn like an unlucky charm, leaving your name facing your body and a blank piece of white paper facing your colleagues.

If you wish to ensure the tag stays where you put it, try a magnetic name tag. You can have one made to suit almost any occasion. These are perfect for "magnetic" personalities, who may want to bring their own name tag. They're very cool—no pins, no paste, no apprehension. One magnet is positioned on the back of your name tag. The other magnet goes under your blouse or shirt.

You may prefer to use the pin-on name tags. Simply apply to the right side of the top of your garment. But here's a warning: if you are wearing delicate fabric, such as silk, avoid those sticky adhesive name tags. Here's another very important tip (and a drycleaner's dilemma): Do not apply sticky name tags to suede. You could have adhesive on your lapel forever and the color could lift off your garment onto the tag upon removal. This could be an expensive mistake!

Stop. Look. Listen. Again, in a busy room, a rushed moment, a social occasion, or business networking session, we may be so distracted by what's going on around us that we "lose" a person's name in the confusion. To help you keep the name safe in your memory, here are some safety tips:

Stop: Yoo-hoo! Over here! Pay attention. Be in the moment when you meet someone new. Try to focus on that person's name and concentrate on his or her name when introduced. Apply both your emotional and physical skills. Remembering names involves your expressions *and* your demonstrative reaction. That means use your communicators: your eyes, mouth, ears, and/or hands.

Look: Use effective eye contact. Do more than *look* at someone. *See* the person's face and notice his or her behavior. Remember something unique and interesting about him or her. Determine whether that person reminds you of someone or something. If you watch for clues, you cannot lose. This applies to any social occasion.

Be on the lookout. Names can remind us fondly of others. Does Betty remind you of another Betty in your life? Perhaps she reminds you of a classic actress like Bette Davis. If so, try to remember to say "Betty" when you see her again.

Facial or body features can prompt memory. Is *Br*enda someone with beautiful *br*own eyes? Just remember the alliteration of "brown eyes" and Brenda's positive facial feature and you may increase your chances of remembering that her name is Brenda.

Environment can prompt name memory by paying attention to the person's surroundings. Does your new neighbor Doug have a lovely landscaped garden? Then think of *Doug* who *digs* or who *dug* in the garden.

Listen: Active listening is more than simply hearing a name. If you apply some positive energy to remembering a new name, you can do it. Make a connection in time and hear the rhyme. Does a name sound similar to a subject, place, or experience? Then, it'll be easy to remember Br*ian* from sc*ien*ce class or *Jim* from the *gym*. Does your new co-worker Sh*irley* come in *early*? You get the idea.

Listen to the pronunciation of unusual names. A new acquaintance will usually give you strong clues about how to pronounce his or her name correctly. As we learn or remember new names, be sure to keep those ears perked for clues. Be a pronunciation parrot. Repeating a name is great feedback. It shows you are listening.

Say the name. Say the name. Say the name. It is often easier if you repeat a new name immediately. This is done during the introduction and throughout the small talk portion of a new conversation. Follow the "rule of three." If you can work it into the conversation, try to repeat the new person's name three times: at the beginning, middle, and end of the conversation. This will allow you to use the power of repetition to your advantage.

Beginning: "It's great to meet you, Deborah." This is respectful to Deborah. She may like to hear her name used in an opening line or two.

Use your listening skills. Most people will introduce themselves with the name they prefer. Repeat the name they like. Perhaps Deborah prefers a nickname. Find out. Does she go by Debbi, Debbie, Debby, Deb, or another abbreviation like Dee? If it is an unusual name, be sure to say it aloud with the person's approval. Ask, "Did I say it correctly?" to respect the person's name and to capture the correct enunciation. If you must write the name, you can show some respect by taking another look at the spelling.

Middle: Now you have said it correctly. So use it again. Try inserting a pleasant phrase, such as, "Thanks for your business card, Deborah . . ." or "Have you had a chance to see the new artwork, Deborah?" There, you used it again.

End: Of course, as you are parting ways at the end of the conversation, you can always try this: "Great meeting you, Deborah . . ." or "Thanks, Deborah. Let's stay in touch." Only use this ending if you intend to communicate with this person beyond this first meeting. If possible, take a minute and jot down where you met the new person somewhere you can relocate it, perhaps on the back of his or her business card.

Of course, I know you!

It's bound to happen: memory lapses, senior moments, and the dreaded name drain. If you find yourself in front of someone you should know and whose name you have forgotten, just ask again, with a touch of humor. Most polite people will see the initial panic in your eyes and they'll be kind enough to offer their names to put you out of your misery. And they'll probably laugh with you! It's really okay to be human. Ask for someone's name again with a smile. You might say, "Have you ever had one of those crazy weeks?" or "Another senior moment!" or "I forgot my husband's name yesterday!"

Try to start a new conversation by saying your name right away. For example, "Hi, I'm John Smith . . ." That at least gives some starting info to the other party. Not traveling alone? Educate your networking partner about the "name game," that is, what to do in name emergencies. Your spouse, relatives, or friends can interject and introduce themselves up front with their names along with their own request for someone else's name. "Hi, I'm Ralph, Laura's nephew. And *you* are?" Ah, now you have a chance to hear the name. A little help from your friends can go a long way.

Name that tone.

Stay positive. By all means, use a positive tone when you are saying someone's name. One of our greatest gifts is our own individual name. We love to hear the sound of it. And oh, what a feeling when our name is remembered correctly.

Be nice. Be sure to say something nice about your new acquaintance's name. Then you can be assured you will remember the name with a complimentary comparison. When using memory prompts, handle them wisely. Think of the person's best qualities. If you try to remember someone's name with a negative feature, like that really *hairy* guy named *Harry*, you might end up offending, then mending a relationship you've worked hard to build!

Often, mutually beneficial relationships begin in business networking situations or social gatherings. Are you using your networking opportunities to your best advantage? With a little rehearsal, you might be amazed at your networking know-how.

CHAPTER 9

Be Positively *Fabulous,* Dahling!
Your Public Awaits

Are you a "positively" professional person? The way you express yourself can affect how your message is received, and that can affect how memorable you are or how well you come across to others. Give yourself an energy boost with a positive image. This chapter will help you understand the importance of communication styles and how they can affect your message.

The power of positive language.

Positive language is energizing. Negative energy is draining. It's been said that it takes more muscles to maintain a frown than to express a simple smile. How exhausting it would be to frown for an entire conversation. What's more, a disheartening look on our faces is contagious. When we talk with negative communication, it can become very fatiguing not only for us, but also for those around us. Soon, people will connect their drained mood with talking to you.

Positive energy, on the other hand, can invigorate you. Think of how you feel when you catch someone smiling at you. Even over the telephone, we can tell if someone is talking from his or her heart. Think about creating a positive image with a "communications mirror." When delivering good news, keep a mirror by the phone to see if you are talking with a smile in your voice. Take a look at yourself. Do you sound just as positive as you look? If so, your positive energy will be reflected back with positive energy. Conversely, negative energy is reflected back to you when you look and/or speak with a negative attitude.

Sound simple? Maybe, but surprisingly enough, many of those who project a negative attitude don't always have something negative to say. Actually, in many cases, they simply give us the impression of being disinterested or detached. They have not learned to turn their phrases and comments into more constructive, positive dialogue. You can improve your chances of projecting a positively professional attitude.

Tune in to your tone. Like a song lyric, people often remember and emotionally react to things you say to them. We tend to remember extremes, that is, the extremely positive or the extremely negative. Speaking with positive words will increase your chances of being memorable in a positive fashion. Be sure to empathize with the listener when you speak in positive terms.

Have a respectful manner. Avoid speaking in a tone of blame or distancing yourself from others with words like, "You know what's wrong with you people?" or "You claim that . . ." or "We fail to understand how you . . ." Try not to use words like, "don't, can't, won't, not my job," or other language that indicates you are unwilling or unable to cooperate. Negative language, even if unintended, can send a poor image out to those around us, and this verbal mismatch may cause disagreements and confusion.

It's called the "no-can-do" attitude. That's when we turn another's request back into *their* problem, not our pleasure to assist. For example, statements such as, "You should have read the instructions," "You could have looked that up in our directory," or "You'll have to call back. I'm busy . . ." can alienate others.

A "can-do" person would say, "I understand your concerns. Of course, it would be my pleasure to help you . . ." or "I don't have that information, but I'll be glad to return your call when I find it for you . . ." or "Allow me direct you to someone who may assist you."

Remember, if you do not agree with someone, it is not necessary to slip into negative language. For instance, when at odds with another's opinion, simply begin your discussion with a positive point of view to set the tone. Try saying, "I respect your opinion. Now allow me to explain our position . . . ," "May we suggest that you (insert your idea) . . . ," or "Here's an option I'd like to share with you . . ." Try initiating a workable quid pro quo such as, "We can help you with (task or effort) if you can send us (necessary paperwork or documentation)." Take care of your needs, too. Allow some wiggle room for *you* to gain something out of this act of goodwill.

Be your own best friend. Your positive phrasing and language can give you the present of goodwill equity—the credit you deserve for doing good things. When you meet new people, it's crucial to create a positive first impression. Then, the next time you come across their path, they may give you credit for that positive action. For instance, a week after you have met someone new, if you are late for a meeting, that person may defend you. If someone mentions your name, your colleague may smile and say, "Yes, I have met her and she seems very responsible (nice, generous, or approachable). Let's wait for her before we start this meeting."

On the other hand, if you were rude in your first encounter, you may have lost some of your goodwill equity and you'll get little to no credit. In that case, they'll be more likely to start that meeting without you! If you don't care about others, they won't care about you.

Give yourself the gift of gab. Keep in mind, your positive language gives great first impressions. It tells what you want or what can be done and appears helpful and encouraging—not formal or routine. It emphasizes positive actions, encourages movement toward positive results, and leaves a lasting positive image.

Open your presents and improve your presence. Use your gifts of new, positive skills. It'll be easier to use affirmative language when you agree with others. Emulate those who you feel create a positive environment or attitude. Add positive phrasing to your daily discussions: "We welcome your business . . . . ," "Thank you for your consideration . . . ," "What an absolute joy meeting you . . . ," "Looking forward to our next opportunity to . . . . ," or "Glad we've agreed to move forward with . . ." Make it merry. The results will make you smile. That's why I supply mirrors in my communications sessions. When my participants think back on their communication skill-builder experiences after the events, they smile.

Make a communication cheat sheet. Make a list of words you enjoy hearing others say to you and insert them into your vocabulary. Begin by writing some positive words in a notebook; then continue using your new word list. Add some new phrases to your email messages and letters and check the responses you receive. Once you have sharpened your skill of writing in positive terms, it will be easier to adjust your spoken language to present a more positive tone.

Begin your new optimistic attitude and approach and you just may be pleasantly, *positively* surprised.

Dimond's Gems

Everyone excels at something.

Be your own cheerleader.

Create confidence.

Give yourself a pep talk. "Rah, rah! Go, you!" A confident attitude speaks volumes before you ever say a word. You may be surprised and even amused if you remind yourself how talented you are. This will give you a positive mindset. Take your focus off what you think you cannot do and target what you know you can do. Everyone excels at something. Be your own cheerleader.

Give others the cheer. Confident people consider, respect, and applaud the talents and strengths of others. They give credit where credit is due. Pay attention and comment on others' achievements or contributions. Allow a conversation to take its own course. This often leads to positive words sent in your direction. When you want a good conversation icebreaker, try a topic that most people will be glad to talk about: career, home, family, education, entertainment, and recreation.

Now hear this! A confident conversationalist is a good listener. A *great* listener knows the value of voice variation and a consistent message. For instance, do you say that you are "happy to be here" with flat delivery or with some positive emotion? Your tone and inflection should match your words. Record your voice and play it back. You might be surprised at what you hear. Your confidence will grow if you know how you sound to others. Put some energy in your voice and you will sound more confident. It may take some practice, but the results can be rewarding.

Look the part. Your confidence goes far beyond your choice of fashion or style. Present a positive appearance and get a positive reaction. Visualize yourself as others see you, from head to toe. Use eye contact to show you're paying attention and keep your body facing those with whom you are speaking. Avoid looking down, hunching over, fidgeting, or trying to "shrink" into the floor. Relax and be yourself so you won't look unnatural or strained. Do what is comfortable for your body to do. When you begin to focus on others, you will start to emote, gesture, and truly look more confident.

Ready, set, grow your confidence! Anticipate your next important meeting, presentation, or social networking event. Visualize yourself as a confident individual. Rehearse the points you want to make and the way you want to present yourself. Critique yourself on camera. Your preparation can reduce the intimidation of new experiences. Support your own strengths and apply your new skills. This takes energy and a dose of courage, but with practice, you'll begin to welcome each new social situation with a strengthened sense of confidence.

Your body's talking. Are you listening?

Believe it or not, as articulate or friendly as our choice of words might be, our total communication skills can become even more effective if we simply have a good talk with our bodies before we walk into our next meeting, presentation, or conversation. Even the most confident communicators benefit from taking a moment to check and re-check the crucial consistent connection between our words (verbal skills) and our ways (nonverbal skills).

No matter how well we converse, it's really our presence or the way we carry ourselves and project our message that leaves our positive lasting impression. So how can we measure our body talk?

The best way to reveal your use of nonverbals in communication is to watch yourself talk on videotape. Simply have a conversation with a colleague with the camera rolling. Pick a topic that interests you, and if you talk long enough, you should forget about the camera and relax. Start with a comfortable topic that makes you smile; then try a more formal discussion, such as a mock job interview.

When you play back the tape, you can see whether or not you maintain proper eye contact and use appropriate body language during the conversation. For instance, do you lean forward or do your eyes light up when you discuss topics you enjoy? Do you look away or at the ceiling when you must come up with difficult facts or figures? Eye contact, hand gestures, facial expressions, and posture can reveal volumes about your attitude and your viewpoint.

The following quick head-to-toe body check may help the next time you want to ensure you have the best shot at improving your personal or professional presence.

Eye contact: The "eyes" have it! Eyes are powerful communicators. They reveal our interest and our attention, or lack thereof. Remember, the more eye contact you reveal, the more interest you show. This display of positive energy will be returned to you and will make you more memorable. Poor eye contact, however, can show a lack of interest, self-confidence, or credibility.

How much is enough? Simply look at people thoughtfully when you are addressing them. Keep your eyes off the ceiling and the floor!

When addressing a crowd, "punctuate" your sentences with good eye contact. Don't look above heads or dart your eyes around the room. You may think you're making a wide range of eye contact with many people. Instead, you probably look a bit shifty—that's *not* the desired effect!

Instead, look into someone's eyes and finish your first sentence while looking at him. Then, seek out another person and finish your next thought while looking at her. Move your eyes from one person to another. Your gaze should be natural, not exaggerated. Although you don't need to count the seconds out loud, timing is everything. Learn to control the length of your look.

Facial expressions: Don't put away that mirror or the video camera just yet. It's time to look at your entire face. Sure, we may be confident on the inside, but do we know how revealing our facial expressions are to the outside world? If we look at ourselves as others do, we might become more motivated to adjust our expressions to match the mood we're trying to convey.

For instance, obviously, when we have good news to share, we should emote appropriately with a smile. Bad news can be conveyed with a look of concern, and affirmation can be shown with a nod. When we use these feedback skills, we communicate effectively. Yet, due to nervousness or distraction, we sometimes do not realize that we are projecting a nervous smile or even a grimace when we have good news to share. Play back your video.

Watch how your face reveals what you are thinking. Then ask yourself, "Do I shake my head 'no' when I say 'yes'?" That's an example of a mismatched nonverbal.

Posture and demeanor: How we carry ourselves involves good use of our entire body, with a focus on the torso. First of all, be comfortable.

Remember, when we lean slightly into others' space, we can show we are engaged by their message and are interested in what they are saying. Again, as in eye contact, try not to go overboard. People have different comfort levels when it comes to their safe personal sphere. Some will tell you by their own body language when you are getting a bit too close. You should be prepared to read your conversation colleagues' reactions and respect each individual's comfort zone.

Arms and hands: Our arms and hands make the gestures we use to raise or lessen the importance of our message. Some of us gesture quite naturally, which can be an effective way to accentuate our attitude or punctuate our points. Others are more at ease with our hands in a more relaxed position, perhaps on our laps or by our sides. When presenting a speech, you may anchor yourself by touching (not grabbing!) the top of the speaker's podium. Find what makes you most comfortable. Feel free to insert a gesture or two when you feel the need to describe or display your enthusiasm about a topic. Again, don't go overboard. Too much use of your arms and hands may actually divert attention from your message.

Legs: The age-old question is, "to cross or not to cross?" If you are relaxed and able to concentrate on your message with your legs crossed, then do so. However, be aware of your hemline, the escalating slit in your skirt, or what's being exposed by the rising hem of your slacks. (Is that your bare leg showing above your socks?) Crossing legs can be effective, but remember to look at yourself in a mirror or on camera to determine if your crossed legs reveal more skin than you intend. Some choose to cross their legs at the ankle, but you must do what is comfortable for you. How do you look standing up? Sitting down? Legs crossed or uncrossed? Do a quick "stand up/sit down" test and find out.

Consider a coach: These quick tips can show the power of videotaping to evaluate how we project ourselves to others. But to prepare for major presentations or events, it is a good idea to meet with a communications coach or trainer to rehearse exactly how you feel and behave in various real-time scenarios. Communications professionals can determine what kind of message your body is projecting and, more importantly, if it is what you intend to communicate. With the assistance of a coach, you not only can see your hand gestures on a TV screen, but you can also get honest feedback on how your handshake feels to others. You don't simply watch your eye contact and facial expressions on the monitor. You also experience what is truly comfortable and natural when someone is gazing back at you.

It is a good practice to step outside ourselves and get a taste of what others see in us. Demonstrate your strengths to others and be ready to embrace the opportunity to improve. Then determine what kind of lasting impression you want to make. Improving your "presence" can be a "present" to yourself. With a little head-to-toe self-evaluation, you can increase your chances of being aware, being sincere, and showing the world your best.

Power up the passion in your presentation.

If you need help sometime, it's good to rhyme! Here's a little ditty for you: *As you prepare to face the public in any formal way . . . put some passion into the things you'll want to do and say.* Simply begin with the age-old feeling of desire—the desire to do well. If you wish you were more effective in your communications skills, then you've already accomplished the first step toward speaking success. If you want *and* need to improve your communications skills to make a positive difference in your personal or professional life, then you have the additional benefit of true desire. Desire can be a great motivator.

Be contagious! To succeed in communicating with our colleagues, family, and friends, we must be motivated. If you believe in what you are saying, others are more likely to reflect this feeling back to you. Try it. The next time to want to emphasize something, say it with enthusiasm. See the reaction on the faces of those looking at you. Hear the inflection in their voices when they respond to you. Feel the response. Are they reflecting your excitement back to you? If so, you are making progress.

Remember this rhyme: If you believe in what you say and do, others will take action, too. If you *don't* show your self-confidence and conviction, others may be turned off or even ignore you completely.

Believe in yourself first. Then, you will have a better likelihood of convincing those around you. Learn to influence others with your passion.

Have a heart. Have a selfless, big-hearted reason to share your information.

State your objective. Hinting around won't get the job done if nobody picks up on your suggestions. Be direct. If you clearly state what you want to say, your messages and ideas will have a much better chance of being noticed.

Add influence to your language. Ask yourself, "What's my mission? Exactly what do I want to say?" Then focus on that and say it with confidence and attitude.

Keep it simple and sincere. Drop your Dialog Danglers©. These are excess words, usually in the form of short questions, unnecessarily added to the end of your statement. These little phrases can be power robbers. They can suggest that you doubt yourself, even if you are just adding the words to soften the blow of a strong statement. They can pulverize your passion.

Try saying these next sentences aloud:

1. "We have a great organization, *don't you agree?*"
2. "We have a great organization, *you know what I mean?*"
3. "We have a great organization, *isn't that right?*"

Now try simplifying the sentence and saying it aloud this way:

4. "We have a great organization!"

All of the above phrases say that the organization is great, yet sentence #4 has more confidence without the weight of the Dialog Danglers©. Try eliminating those draining danglers whenever possible and you can strengthen your message. Remember to think of your audience first. Be prepared to follow up on your passionate statement with the reasons why you are so enthusiastic. You must create a need to know about your superb organization.

Passion is powerful.

Your energy and commitment to your organization, your family, your mission, your business, or anything you believe can be expressed with power and passion. If you communicate a strong message that is helpful to the audience, that's positive. If you get carried away with overconfidence, you are simply boasting, and that's negative. Every day, each of us has the opportunity to present ourselves in a memorable fashion using our own individual style. How you express yourself with passion begins and ends with your particular comfort level.

Think about the passion you radiate in your message and choice of words—from addressing private or networking meetings to large audiences. Your passionate belief in your message will give you just the boost you may need. Offer something worthwhile that others will need or want to hear. With a little bit of passion, you may achieve what you desire. Make your audience as involved and engaged as *you* are!

Be gone with the wind.

Toward the end of your presentation, interview, negotiation, networking, or social time, find a natural lull in the action and begin making your move to leave.

Breeze outa there. Develop a powerful parting statement that repeats your message. Remind others of your cause. Focus attention back onto your goal. Repeat your name or the name of your company or organization as you end your presentation or conversation, such as, "I'm looking forward to helping you Secure *your* Dynamic Message with Soni Dimond Media." You may be interested to know, I do live what I lecture.

PART THREE

Enrich Your Pitch

CHAPTER 10

Tweaking Your Public Speaking
Don't Be Afraid—Seek Aid!

You've read this. You've heard it said. So it must be true. They (whoever *they* are) say the awesome fear of public speaking exceeds the average human's fear of death. Do you really believe that discouraging information? You certainly don't want to take the front stage and die up there.

Relax. You will not die of embarrassment. So simply get over it! Throw yourself a lifeline. Seek aid through information and practice.

At some point in our lives, each of us becomes a spokesperson. Facing a group, an audience, or the public can be a daunting task. If you dread the idea of public speaking, this part of the book will help you conquer your anxieties, captivate your audience, and build your confidence.

For nearly two decades in the communications business, I've helped competent, interesting people overcome their anxieties about speaking to an audience. Happily, I've found that this "audience anxiety" or "podium phobia" could be overcome and eventually avoided if the same competent, interesting people would only practice a few simple steps toward self-assurance.

In my media training classes, which prepare professionals to be effective, dependable spokespersons, I teach the common-sense approach to speaking in public venues, addressing audiences of all types and sizes and conducting news interviews. Amazingly, once the fear of the unknown is conquered, the key to your effective delivery is as simple as describing yourself with the **ABC's**: Available, Believable, and Consistent.

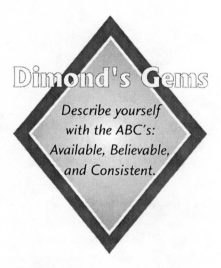

Dimond's Gems

Describe yourself with the ABC's: Available, Believable, and Consistent.

◊ Are you **available** to the media or your public when they need you?

◊ Is what you say **believable**? Do you sound well informed?

◊ How **consistent** are you? If you want to be recognized as consistently credible, beef up your bio to show that you are an expert, pundit, author, speaker, or the top company spokesperson. Ask yourself, "What's in my personal or professional skills stockroom?" Then ask, "Am I displaying those skills in society's showroom?"

Play up your strengths.

Put away your uneasiness. We'll work under the assumption that you already possess certain attributes and that your audience will benefit by your effective application. Let's get started with the "Eight Steps Toward Speaking Success."

1. **Know who are you and why you are there.** Perception is reality. Let's start with our appearance. When we look good, we feel confident. If we feel confident, we will be confident. Know the audience and dress appropriately. This comfort level is important as we prepare to stand in front of others.

    Before you decide what you are going to say, find out as much as you can about where your remarks will take place and who is going to listen to what you have to say. How do you want them to remember you? Think of ways your audience can benefit from your knowledge. Take this opportunity to be an expert, pundit, or spokesperson. They'll need what you know. Prepare for your presentation with a strong opening and an impressive closing. Those first and last lines are the most memorable and may be what influence your audience; so make those precious words powerful.

2. **Know thy audience.** Simply know the audience rules! "It's not all about you." If I repeat that phrase throughout the book, it's definitely on purpose. Take the focus off of yourself and redirect your attention to the audience. They will help you establish the appropriate tone. Find out what information they want to hear from you. As we like to say in the speaking business: What's the audience's favorite radio station? WII-FM! (What's In It-For Me?) Give 'em news they can use and deliver it in their tone.

    If you know exactly what you want to share with them, tune-up your talk to include the most frequently asked questions about that topic. If you're not sure what a particular audience might want to hear, talk with the person who is running the show, occasion, program, or conference. Find out more about who's going to listen to you. It's all about them. Customize your tone and delivery to meet their needs. Good presentations build audience awareness. Great presentations build audience rapport.

3. **Take a look in the mirror. Do you like what you see?** Try to keep your closet up-to-date with at least one suit or outfit that looks particularly good on you every time you wear it. You should not have to have a panic attack each time you need to decide what to wear. Have those smart-looking outfits hanging in your closet, dry cleaned and ready to wear. These are your "no-brainer" outfits.

    My friends in retail have helped update my closet with this advice: You shouldn't have to think too hard to know which clothes will work for you. When it's five o'clock in the morning and you must rush to catch a plane, those "no-brainers" are essential! The faster you're over the hurdle of what you should wear, the more time you will have to focus on your day, your schedule, and of course, your message.

    When selecting your attire, remember to respect your audience enough to know what they expect from you. If it is a casual gathering, present yourself in a casual manner. If it's a formal affair, be more formal.

    You must develop a "camera eye." It's how others see you and your every move. (I have stressed this previously, but it is extremely important.) Picture your movements as if you were on camera. Be aware of the way you stand, sit, and walk. At random points throughout your speech, picture a "freeze-frame" of your gestures. That's what a photo of you would look like. Notice where your hands are and how you cross your legs. Examine your facial expressions. How do you look in this freeze-frame position? Do you like what you see? If you need to improve that image, adjust your posture, change your facial expression, and sit or stand in a style that's comfortable, but not contrived. Then practice your freeze-frame rehearsal again.

4. **Know what you want to say and how you want to say it.** Your message is the most important thing. It is the center of attention. You are the carrier of this message; so naturally, the speech you give should not be about you. It should be about your message. You must be able to relay your message to your audience.

You must be believable. As a spokesperson, you know that you must distill your message to convey the major points that are the basis of your speech. If you haven't brought your written, verbatim speech, at least have your note cards within reach as a guide for you to address your points and control your content and your delivery.

All jokes aside. If you are tempted to start your speech with a joke or a funny story, you might want to think again, especially if you are not a natural comic or storyteller. Before you launch into a stand-up routine, ask yourself, "Is this story appropriate for the audience? Is this story in good taste? Would I want someone to repeat this story with my name attached to it?"

Don't make excuses for your performance. These heavy opening words will weigh you down. For instance, do not begin your speech with, "I'm sorry to take your time." This "sorry" phrasing begs the question, "So why are we listening to you if you are really sorry? Do you think this is a waste of our time?"

Instead, speak with authority. Effective self-expression requires a fearless mindset. Of course, this is easier said than done. Perhaps, the best advice is to get over whatever "they" say and don't let 'em see you sweat . . . or shake . . . or stammer. Ask yourself, "How can I be afraid of this audience?" The answer may be that you don't know most of them, and if you're like most of your colleagues, you probably fear the unknown. In many cases, the audience is in your corner. They are in the room to learn something from you. The more you focus on them, the more familiar they will become to you. Soon, you'll become more at ease. (Need more help? See Chapter 11 for stage fright tips!)

Give positive energy and you will get positive energy in return. Be glad you are presenting. Be glad they are listening. Be concerned about their needs. Show them what you know and why they need your information, perspective, or skills.

Practice emoting appropriately. Feel free to relax your expression. It's appropriate to smile when delivering good news. Deliver more serious points with a more serious expression. Because you are communicating with the power of your voice, your inflection is important. Hitting words with a slightly louder or stronger voice will emphasize the points you wish to make. To catch your listeners' attention, pause—between—major thoughts to "lift" them from a series of comments.

(If I were presenting this as a speech to a group, I would pause here . . .)

Your audience will want to know one thing about your message. Remember their favorite radio station, WII-FM? Good! Because they'll be thinking, "What's in it-for me?" When talking with the media, relate your message to the reading, listening, or viewing audiences' concerns.

Do you have a "news hook"? A news hook is a descriptive way to say your particular message "hooks" into today's headlines and breaking news. Read the newspaper, watch TV, and listen to the radio. Be aware of what is making news. If you can do this, you will make your message relevant and important to your audience.

5. **Become a credible, reliable source.** During both good and challenging times, if *you* don't believe in what you say, why should your audience? Know your audience and address them confidently, using short statements and direct quotes. Use the words "you" and "we." Bring them into your world and let them feel good, bad, provoked, inspired—anything

you want; but your message should address them as real people. They took time and trouble to hear what you have to say. If you don't care about your audiences' needs, you are not respecting them. If you are not respectful, they will turn you off.

You can learn to turn an unreceptive audience around with essential skills rooted in respect. If they don't necessarily like what you say, at least they will be more likely to honor your right to say it. And, when being interviewed by a reporter or addressing questions from your audience, remember to honor his or her opinion, even if you disagree.

If you are conducting a series of speeches or interviews, you should be delivering a customized and consistent message to your audiences. If your message alters, be proactive about getting the word out. Notify the media or the organization of the updated information.

6. **Got a message? Make it snappy.** Don't derail your train of thought. Once you've developed your consistent message, make sure you can get your point or points across. A good way to remember this lesson is to boil down your broad message to its simplest form. This is often called "distilling" the message.

No matter how complicated you may think your issue is, remember: a television or radio interview will only allow a few seconds for you to get your point(s) across. It's a tried and true fact that you will lose your audience's attention after twenty minutes. Great speeches of our time have been delivered in much less time. The Gettysburg Address was eloquent, memorable, and delivered in only a few short minutes. A brief, to-the-point speech doesn't allow much time to ramble on and get sidetracked.

Being interviewed for TV or radio? You will have certain words or expressions you'll want to highlight in your remarks. Practice your applause lines (where you want them to clap for you), favorite phrases, and sound bites. Due to society's lack of attention span, good sound bites require timing. Are your quotes fewer than ten seconds long? If so, that's good. But, it may not be good enough. Keep trying try to say your quote (without slurring words or racing) until you can say something pithy in fewer than seven seconds. Now you're talkin' for TV!

Run through your remarks several times. Break down your top points and give yourself the power of the pause (*puh-lease*, take a breath) after seven seconds. This takes practice, but it increases your chances of producing a phrase worth quoting.

Since the first days of communications training sessions, coaches have emphasized the importance of showing your audience your joy, concern, compassion, and authority. Keep your message simple enough to understand, interesting enough to hold their attention, and compelling enough to leave them with the desire to know more.

7. **Rehearse, rehearse, and (did I mention?) rehearse your speech.** Break down the word "rehearse" to the phrase "re-hear." That's the value of practicing your delivery. None of us can know exactly how we present ourselves and our message to others unless we examine how others hear and see us.

"Hear ye! Hear ye!" How do you sound to others? Is your message getting across? Do you find your delivery interesting or could you spice it up with better inflection or projection? Record your voice to hear what the audience hears and make adjustments accordingly.

See yourself as others do. It's an "out of body" experience. To find out how you appear to others, look in a three-way mirror to see how you look from the front and back, standing up and sitting down. Then videotape your presentation to see how you look in action.

"Bridges" can help guide you through Question and Answer (Q & A) sessions. Try to make three points in your presentation. It gives you a chance to return to a "safe place" (your point) when you begin to feel sidetracked. A few, well-selected salient points will assist you in controlling any follow-up interviews or Q & A periods.

Review your answers to potential queries from the audience or questions from the media. (For more on the news media's needs, check out Chapter 12: "The Media Pitch.")

It's useful to practice what you can do if you are thrown off-guard by a question. Learn the art of "bridging" back to the three points you want to make. Practice saying a few lines such as, "That's certainly one opinion, but I'd like to share this idea with you," or "That's another topic altogether. Thanks for bringing it to our attention, yet let's first be sure to examine the point of today's discussion." Soon you will find out how easy it is to control the interview. Of course, I must remind you to always bridge back to your message with honesty and respect.

If someone is asking an intriguing, yet irrelevant question after your speech, politely refer him or her elsewhere. You can do this by saying, "Interesting question. You deserve a complete answer to that. I'd be glad to discuss it with you after this presentation . . ." or "There's been a lot of attention to that matter, I agree. We've been following that issue, along with what we're discussing today. Let me explain." Then remember to segue back to your main point.

Don't take the *bait*, if someone is *luring* you off message. Stay on message! Your message must stand alone, with the inflection and words you wish to say, not the words, phrases or baited lines others may try to feed you. As you rehearse your delivery and your responses to questions, remember to avoid repeating a "loaded question." These loaded questions are inquiries full of words that you may wish to avoid. Once you've said them, those words can be quoted and attributed to you. Resist the urge to repeat those accusatory or negative words, even if you're trying to deny them. As they say in the news business, "Nothing's off the record."

8. **Be a real person before you are a spokesperson.** Humanize your message. It's okay to be yourself. Just show the public your best! Take a moment before you answer. Think before you speak. Visualize what you say as a headline or a sound bite on the air. You might find that you are not being as eloquent as another speaker, but you do possess strengths of your own. So play to those strengths and win over your audience.

    Allow the audience to see you as a person who can be spontaneous and not over-polished. If your microphone drops off of your lapel or if your hair falls in your eyes, take it lightly. Did you spill coffee on your jacket? No worries. No one expects you to be perfect. If you are simply yourself, a human with faults and idiosyncrasies, you may receive more audience empathy and identification. As long as you can laugh at yourself, your audience or the interviewer will understand your dilemma.

    Use your good manners. Be respectful and thank the audience and/or reporters for the opportunity to have been heard. Remember the golden rule of public speaking: giving positive energy increases your chance of receiving positive energy. Although there's no guarantee of a remarkable reception, your audience will treat you as well as you treat them.

Whether you are teaching a class, presenting a training session, speaking to a social group, hosting an event, or facing the media, apply these communications skills during your next public appearance. You now have the power to manage your message. Videotape your performance or speech and watch—really watch! Are you pleased, proud, or puzzled? Chances are, you'll be surprised at what presentation potential you have.

CHAPTER 11

The Scared Pitch Project
Stage Fright is All in Your Head . . .
Your Mouth . . . Your Chest . . .
Your Hands . . . .

The wind blows and whips outside. The lights are down low and there's a creepy, cold chill that goes straight up your spine. A voice in the distance calls your name. Are you having a nightmare?

No. You are being called to the front of the room to deliver a speech. Gulp.

Now that you've prepared and rehearsed your content, tone, and style, it's time to take center stage.

If the thought of getting up to speak in front of a group of strangers makes your bones shudder, you are not alone. The trick is to fight the fright. But how?

Like it or not, life requires us all to "perform" now and then. Facing the public can be a daunting task, whether we must deliver a toast at a wedding or present a proposal to the Board of Directors. I've developed Fluster Busters© to help you learn to enjoy public speaking. They will guide you in reducing stress and experiencing more success.

Fluster #1—What's that scary sound in your chest? Thump, thump, thump . . .

Hmmm—is that your telltale heart? Not so, Edgar Allan Po-dium! Your heart may be pulsing at warp speed as you stand at the podium, but believe it or not, you are the only one who can hear it beating. It's something you can feel more than hear. It's your body's call to action. This apparently involves adrenaline and that fight-or-flight issue. You are involuntarily taking your heart rate over its speed limit.

Buster #1: Slow down. Your body needs some air!

You may be holding your breath a bit, since you are oh, so nervous. So open your mouth and breathe. That's it. Slowly and comfortably . . . breathe in, then breathe out. I'll bet you already know how to do this exercise, since you've probably been doing it your whole life.

After you regulate your breathing, you may concentrate on the important thing in front of you: the audience. Turn your attention to someone who is giving you a positive look. Return the glance with a nod or smile. Center yourself at the front of the room and take your time.

If you are following another speaker, be aware of the placement of the microphone. Move it up or down to meet the level of your mouth and stand in a secure position. If the podium is too high for you, twist the mic to the side (or remove and hold it) and stand beside the podium. Help the audience hear you, see you, and respect you. How can they do all that if you are barely peaking over the podium? If you are truly not sure if they can see you, then ask them! The audience will tell you. This gives you a chance to begin interacting with your attendees right from the start. You are in control. You can set the mood and the pace. Make this experience positive.

As you become more absorbed and involved in the comfort of the audience, you should begin to feel your heart rate come back to a normal beat. Remember, the audience needs what you know.

Fluster # 2: What's embarrassed and red all over? Could it be you?

If your face and neck begin to blotch like a bad makeover and you feel your cheeks getting hot, you may be suffering from what happens when there's a significant change in the blood flow to your outer skin layers. Again, you are feeling the results of the physical rush of stage fright. Once you've shown your true colors, people in the audience can tell you're scared. Of course, most reasonable people will understand how you feel and will empathize completely. Even though we've all been embarrassed at least once, this "face on fire" shade may not be your most attractive look, so let's nip it in the blush.

Buster #2: Focus on your good manners and getting the red out.

If the hot seat is making you a rosy shade of red, you should know it's usually only a temporary condition. Mercifully, this "stage fright scarlet" usually doesn't last very long.

Everyone has experienced feeling a bit flush, so overcome the obvious redness by relaxing into something that makes the audience smile. This is not the time to deliver an opening joke, though. Merely start your speech by thanking the host, hostess, or organization. Take the focus off of you at the top of the talk. This opening of thanks will soften your tone and put you in control of your comfort zone. It also speaks well of your manners. Thanking the host for giving you the floor is a positive beginning to even the most controversial topics. The more thanks you reveal, the less flushed you'll feel.

Fluster # 3: Honey, who shrunk my vocal cords? It's the return of the dreaded dry mouth and disappearing voice dilemma.

Hey, what's happening? You were okay just a second ago. You might have begun the meeting with a voice. Now it's gone. You are finally called to the stage and suddenly your mouth feels like it's been vacuumed. It seems like cotton has collected on your gums and even your lips feel swollen and stuck together. You begin to mumble as you fumble for what's left of your tongue. Again, that sneaky, sinister stage fright has invaded your space. It's another likely side effect to what's going on inside your panic-stricken body.

Buster #3: No voice? No problem. Hydrate and concentrate.

Remember to revive your saliva. Try to bring water with you if your host has not provided it for you at the podium. Stop a moment and sip. Swoosh it in your mouth for a moment before you swallow. Get those glands back in action.

If there is no liquid refreshment available to you, enjoy a mint before speaking. Mints can bring some life back into your lips, tongue, and mouth. Try to avoid chewing gum, since you may forget to take it out of your mouth (ugh). Then once onstage, there'll be no place to put it. Chomping can distract the audience and it's not pretty. Imagine the horror of later seeing yourself munching on camera if they tape your presentation. When it comes to gum, chew it on your own time, not in front of an audience. When in doubt, take it out.

So before going on stage, enjoy a mint, sip a beverage, and relax a moment. Take comfort in regaining control of your senses. If you had a voice just a moment ago, your voiceless condition is indeed temporary. This condition often happens within seconds of that radiant red face fiasco and it disappears as quickly.

Dimond's Gems

*Want
"silence of the limbs"?*

*Control those
terrible trembling
appendages.*

Fluster # 4: Want *Silence of the Limbs?* Take control of those terrible, trembling appendages.

It's not cold, yet you are shivering. If you are naturally calm and collected, but in front of an audience, your hands, knees, and feet unexpectedly begin to bobble around, you may have the "stage fright shakes." You grab for the podium, but now you are wobbling it from side to side. You put one hand in your pocket, then the other hand in your other pocket, but you can't find a place to put those twitching fingers. The more you try to stop it, the more violently you begin to quiver. Your knees knock, your hands tremble. It's distracting to both you and the audience. How do you stop the stage fright shakes?

Buster #4: Return to your relaxed self.

Your stage-frightened body can become a ball of nervous energy. It can quickly become too much for you to handle because your circulation and breathing have altered and you're slightly out of control. You may want to try this combo platter of concentration exercises: Stand or sit straight, with good posture. Hold your pose. Tighten the muscles a bit; then slowly loosen up all your muscles as you look out into the audience.

It's amazing! You can feel your circulation returning. Remember to slowly breathe in and breathe out. Try to let go of anything that can wobble or make noise, such as the podium, your notes, your bracelet, the change in your pocket, etc. Center yourself and concentrate on the audience and what they need. Focus on your friends in the audience, not your frenzies.

More Fluster Busters© "Do's and Don'ts"

Remember, what works for one speaker will not always be the key to success for another.

Do strategize. Know what you'll be wearing for the presentation. If you have the luxury of preparing several days or weeks ahead of the event, have your clothing clean and ready to wear. And don't be a wrinkled mess! If you're staying in a hotel, send the outfit to the housekeeping staff to be cleaned and pressed. You'll be feeling more confident when you face the crowd and it'll take the stress out of dressing for speaking success.

Do familiarize. Being sensational starts with being conversational. Talk as if you already know your audience. Get to know your attendees and what they will want to know. Don't give them **TMI** (**Too Much Information**). Respect their need to know and believe in what you're saying. You might want to change some words to match the speech the audience uses. For instance, casual gatherings require more casual words and phrasing while formal events require a well-mannered delivery. Transform your speech by relating an appropriate and meaningful message to the audience.

Do energize. Pre-event stress can be draining. Pick up your energy level a bit and rehearse to re-hear your own words. Read the speech back before you give it. Emphasize your key words. Record yourself. Play it back. Listen to your rehearsal. Do you think your presentation is interesting? How can you enliven it to meet the needs of your listeners? Your audience will know immediately if you are interested in your own message. If you are interesting, they'll be interested.

Do personalize your preparation. The key to good Fluster Busters© is to know what is normal for you. Then you can relax and control it to make it work for you. For instance, with stage fright's resulting higher body temperature, some people perspire much more than others. If you do, bring a tissue, an absorbent wipe, or handkerchief for quick, necessary touch-ups on your forehead, above your lip, and around your neck. If the tissue is treated, check the contents of the absorbent papers to be sure you are not wiping away your perspiration with anything that'll make you break out in a rash. Then move on and focus on your presentation, not your perspiration.

Don't try to disguise your symptoms. If you feel faint or if you have constant physical side effects when you speak in public, consult a physician immediately. Be honest with yourself if you feel unusual or ill. As in most exercises, Fluster Busters© tips respect people's boundaries and limitations.

Don't be frightened by feedback. If you're wondering, "How am I doing?" then remember to breathe. Pause and look around the room for audience feedback. Your attendees will show you when they are interested in what you are saying. Feedback tells you if they are lost, confused, or alienated. Acknowledge an occasional laugh or a nod as you speak. This will increase your comfort level, heighten the natural tone of your voice, and improve your posture.

Don't prolong your presentation. No matter how interesting your speech, know when enough is enough. Respect the time constraints of busy schedules and short attention spans and your audience will thank you.

With these tools, you may find public speaking is not scary at all. And with practice, you may overcome your fear enough to enjoy a return trip to the podium after your first success in front of the big, but not-so-scary room!

CHAPTER 12

Toss A Good News Pitch
Catch the Media's Attention

I t is essential for you to realize the difference between advertising and news, or "earned media." When you buy your publicity, it is rightfully dubbed paid advertising. Earned media is free (no monetary charge), but you must be proactive and prove your story to be newsworthy—worthy of news coverage. You can gain as much, or sadly, as little publicity as you know how to earn. Earned media is not guaranteed. Are you are familiar with the old saying, "When it bleeds, it leads?" It's simply human nature. We need to know about controversy, conflict, and chaos. Bad news or breaking news can bump your good news story right off the airwaves or headlines.

You can discover or even create your own newsworthy stories or events, but you must know the rules to gain this kind publicity.

News coverage is not bought, it is earned. Therefore we call it "earned media." By properly offering the stories to news reporters, editors, and producers in your media market, you can generate effective coverage that targets specific audiences with your message. Here are some tips to help you benefit from your potential news media coverage.

Dimond's Gems

*News is not bought.
It is earned.*

Determine your hook (the news bait).

Answer these questions with "Yes" or "No."

Yes   No   Does your story relate to a current fad, trend, or event?

Yes   No   Is your event unusual, or a first of its kind?

Yes   No   Is your story interesting to the public outside of your walls?

Yes   No   Does your story involve the community through acts of kindness and charity?

Yes   No   Do you have a story that is amusing or entertaining?

Yes   No   Can you link your story with a calendar event, such as a holiday or anniversary?

Check your answers. If you answered "Yes" to any of the above, you might have a news hook. If you answered "No," then your story is more news*letter*-worthy than newsworthy. What's in it for the readers or viewers? Write for the end-user.

Valuable news coverage should not be a thinly-veiled ad. Again, remember: Ads are bought. News coverage is earned. News stations often run this phrase: "News you can use!" Earned media is best when it's usable information for the audience (readers, viewers, or listeners).

Your company, organization, or cause may wish to share a wealth of fascinating information. However, if you have details that only your clients or members can appreciate, you may have more of a newsletter than a news report.

Wind up and pitch!

News media professionals expect a pitch that is unusual, distinctive, useful, practical, timely or ahead of its time, and loaded with a local news angle. They expect a news pitch that is not mistaken for an ad or sales presentation. It should contain content that is different from the countless other pitches newsrooms receive. It must also include current contact information with reliable names and phone numbers.

Shore up your news pitch with a **DUNE!** Your pitch should be:

◊   Dynamic
◊   Unique
◊   New
◊   Exciting

Less is more. Time is precious in a newsroom. Keep your pitch short and to the point. Reporters, editors, and producers receive calls and emails pitching stories every week. Although some can be friendly and receptive to phone pitches, expect others to be intolerant, due to so many calls and pending deadlines. Expect to be cut off unless you can grab the news professionals' attention at the right time. Recognize and respect their time and deadlines.

Know your target media's deadlines. Contact the print and broadcast media in your market to inquire about their story deadlines. Does your area have both a morning and evening newspaper? If so, determine when the reporters can accept verbal pitches. Find out if local television and radio stations have morning producers' meetings. Your call should be placed during the time of day when newsrooms are not in pre-show, high-energy modes. Unless it's breaking news, a crisis, or an emergency, avoid making late afternoon pitches to TV newsrooms that run 4:00 p.m., 5:00 p.m., 6:00 p.m., or 11:00 p.m. broadcasts.

If you want to place your story in a magazine, know that they have long front-end deadlines. You may need to pitch a story several months in advance. Find out how much lead time they will need on a placement.

Collect your information, then call only at appropriate times. You may find through your research that some news professionals would rather review pitch letters with additional, pertinent information enclosed before they receive your pitch call.

Remember the media's needs.

Wow 'em with your enthusiasm. Don't bury your lead by layering your pitch with too many details. Pitch with your most exciting news up front. Then back it up with substance, such as statistics, directions, sponsors, point persons, spokespeople, and other specific information.

Be ready. Have your five "W's" of who, what, where, when, why, and sometimes your "H" for how, ready before you call the media. Think about what the media is listening for when receiving your pitch.

◊   Radio needs sound bites (audio).
◊   TV needs footage (video).
◊   Newspaper needs headlines, quotes, and photos.

Provide current and reliable contact info. Secure a name and phone number for the media to contact if they have questions or concerns. If you are the best contact, then you must give both office and cell numbers where you may be reached. Have reliable spokespeople, who can be easily reached and will talk to the media, ready to take calls. Provide spokespeople with talking points. They should know the five W's and the H.

Pitch-hunt. Look for everything that can make your pitch memorable and meaningful. Assemble your pitching points and have them in front of you when you make the call. Politely agree to call back if the reporter, editor, or producer sounds otherwise occupied.

Pitch a clear, concise message if you get voicemail. State your name, number, and why you called—not your life story. Don't "build the clock" for them. Just "tell them the time"—or the place, or the reason for the event, your mission, or public message.

Deliver a slow pitch. Spell any difficult names. This will help avoid confusion (was that *Bill* or *Will?*) Carefully enunciate your contact information to the reporter who needs it to call back.

Practice perfect pitch. Say that pitch out loud. Are you interesting or do you need to condense your sentences? Can you make your pitch short, sweet, and memorable? If not, practice until you can say it in less than a minute.

Don't pad your pitch. Avoid using acronyms or slang, even if you think it's obvious what you mean.

Be a pitch doctor. Find the cure. If the reporter asks a question you are unprepared to answer, tell him you will call him back with further information. Never assume or guess what the media needs.

Don't ditch the pitch. Got turned down? Don't give up too easily or too quickly. If you are rejected in your first pitch, find out if there is someone else in the newsroom (a beat reporter, a feature reporter, health reporter, you name it) who'd find your pitch fascinating.

Throw a fast pitch. Quickly, get alternate contact information and prepare to pitch again. But first, be sure to thank the person with whom you are speaking and make a graceful, positive, expedient exit.

Hit the proper pitch. Make a good lasting impression. You never know when your media paths will cross again.

Be prepared to catch a pitch. Be available. Develop a consistently positive relationship. Let the media know they can call you back. Let them count on you to provide usable information to them when *they* need it, not only when *you* need it.

PART FOUR

The Ceremonial Pitch

CHAPTER 13

Your Opening Pitch

Make Toasts That Don't Burn

D o you find yourself in a panic as you prepare to share a few words in a toast to the graduate, a bride and groom, an award recipient, or to celebrate a special occasion? Make your next toast a "piece of cake."

The toast: a treat not a treatment.

Let's have a toast! Throughout centuries, the toast has become a key component of social communication. It is a signal that an event or happy occasion, and the participants' mood, is progressing from formal to more informal. A toast is an opportunity to express emotion, good cheer, and positive sentiments. It is usually the last activity before the fun begins. So if possible, make *your* toast tasty: short, sweet, and superbly memorable.

Hosts and hostesses: plug in your toasters!

How many times have you heard the poor, unfortunate soul who begins his toast with: "Sorry, I'm not prepared. Wow, I didn't know I had to give a toast. Oh well, here goes nothin' . . ." (and it usually is)? Do yourself and your guests a favor: Avoid the dreaded crowd cringe. Notify your toasters.

A good host knows that to keep the event a pleasant one, he must choose those who will toast wisely, with respect to the type of occasion it is and the audience's limited attention span. Well in advance of the special occasion, let the official toaster(s) know how honored you'd be if they'd address the crowd at your wedding, graduation, or social gathering. They'll be grateful for the heads-up and chances are, your hand-selected colleagues will be glad to do their homework and prepare.

Toast for everyone.

Hosts should prepare for occasional, unscripted moments of freelance toasting. It's wonderful for guests of honor to be toasted by several people in the room, but be wise and appoint an MC (Master or Mistress of Ceremonies) to keep you distanced from the decision-making. Your MC will be prepared to handle requests and schedule changes with grace and charm. He will manage the official rounds of toasts and can identify and introduce any extra speakers who want to give their own toasts.

If the MC is on a tight time frame, he should identify those "instant toasters" who are not scheduled to speak during the formal agenda, and allow special time for a few words to be said after the main event.

Of course, all well-wishers are appreciated, yet impromptu toasters must be sure to respect the host's agenda and time schedule. Remarks should be kept brief, positive, heartfelt, respectful, and courteous.

Light toast.

A good toast is light on length but heavy on happiness and hope. The event's guests will thank you for saying your memorable sentiments in approximately three minutes. Think of light thoughts, such as the recipient's best qualities. Use adjectives and phrases that describe those qualities and how those traits affect this special occasion.

Practice your toast.

Practice your short speech before the event so the words come out naturally. Anything extra you'd like to add to your remarks can be written in a card or slipped into your gift.

Tips for tasteful toasts:

Before you launch into your toast, review this simple checklist:

1. Be sure everyone has a filled glass before you start.
2. Use the hosts' or honorees' names in the toast.
3. Tell the guests who *you* are.
4. Lead the audience with easy directions, such as, "Please rise and stand with me to honor Robert and Roberta . . ."
5. Raise your glass.
6. Keep your glass raised throughout the toast. (This is one reason to keep your speech short!)
7. Face and lead the crowd to set the tone for the room. The audience will mirror your actions.

Begin and end with your sentiments. For instance: "What a celebration for all of us who know this happy couple." Pause and smile. "This day is particularly meaningful to me. As a childhood friend of this beautiful bride, who I admire in so many ways . . ." Make eye contact with the person you are toasting and insert a few good words about his or her family, as well.

Put a personal story in the middle. Insert poignant memories, especially ones that are lighthearted or humorous. Share the sentiments of everyone who cares about the toast recipients.

Be relevant and respectful. Marvelous marriage toasts include a respectful phrase for both the bride (let's call her "Bridela") and the groom ("Groomert"), with best wishes and congratulations to the couple. For example: "I remember how Bridela described her first impressions of Groomert. As some of you know, they met in gourmet cooking class." Then tell a short version of that story. "And I'm sure all of you who know Groomert will agree, not only can he cook, he also has excellent taste!" Pause again, look at the bride. Smile and see the audience lighten up with you. After that, raise your glass, look at the couple, and finish with, "Here's to the happy couple, Groomert and Bridela!"

The most gracious graduation and award toasts include a nod to the recipient's hard work, dedication, and drive to succeed. Show the recipient as an example for others to follow. Insert a personal story if you have one. For instance, "Here's to the woman whose patience helped me complete my first science project and whose wisdom made sure I didn't blow up the chemistry lab! Jane, I always knew you'd be a leader in the pharmaceutical research field. You have a natural ability to share your knowledge with others. I know you'll use your skills to improve lives in so many ways. Here's to your productive future. Here's to *you*, Jane."

Butter-up the toast.

Avoid embarrassing stories. Keep any references to the past flattering and in good taste. This is a time to see the recipient shine.

Sharing toasts.

You may lessen the stress of coming up with something clever to say by citing literature or adding a line from a favorite poem, but be sure to give the author appropriate credit. People appreciate well-selected, relevant quotes.

Don't milk the toast.

Know when enough is enough already! Follow a structure for your toast so it doesn't get bogged down in TMI, or way Too Much

Information (Remember TMI from Chapter 11?) Read your toast aloud, then ask yourself, "Is this too long? Will the audience relate? Do I need that story, joke, or anecdote?" When in doubt, cut it out.

A good toast is brought to a natural finish with a formal indication, such as, "Now please join me in a toast to love, long life, and joy," or "To the happy couple!" or "Here's to Mr. and Mrs. Newlywedson!"

Raise your glass to everyone. Alert the room and they will follow your lead. You may want to say "Cheers!" or any short line you want the guests to repeat. Then "clink" or make the "tip and clink" air gesture. Or if possible, clink your glass against the recipient's glass. Then the guests will tip and clink, too. Next, simply sip. The guests will sip with you. Smile at the recipient and be sure to share your smile with others.

Dimond's Gems

Pop up to give the toast.

Sit down to be served the toast.

Pop up to give the toast. Sit down to be served the toast.

Whenever possible, toasters rise to give a toast; recipients sit to receive a toast. If you are receiving the toast, you are not expected to raise your glass. After you have received the toast, be sure to thank the toaster. Then you may raise your glass in appreciation or gesture to show your gratitude, and take a sip after the toaster.

There are variations on this theme. It is generally advised to wait an appropriate length of time before you extend any gestures. Do what is comfortable for you. Respecting your audience is the key. Make sure your toaster knows you were touched by the kind words.

There are many books and guidelines that describe when to toast, how to toast, and why to toast. But from experience we can say, there's no wrong way to say thank you if you are sincere. Whatever you do with *respect* is *correct*.

Now, please join me in a "hip, hip, hooray!" to the readers of this book. May you have many happy occasions to use your toasting skills. Here's to you! (Clink!)

CHAPTER 14

Cheering or Jeering
How to Play Nice at Parties

I f you find polite party conversation a challenge instead of cheer, these conversation etiquette tips may help you serve your guests—and yourself well.

Thankfully, many of us have wonderful, warm and loving families and friends. Yet, there is always a moment (or several) during a holiday or special occasion gathering when our manners are put to the test.

If you find yourself less than jolly during holiday seasons or family gatherings, do yourself a favor: Be nice. Think twice. Pause a moment. Be calm and centered before you are tempted to respond. If your ultimate goal is to keep the event a joyful experience, use non-threatening, friendly words when you talk. Sometimes, say nothing. When timed appropriately, your silence can speak volumes.

To help ensure you're content at events and happy at the holidays, give yourself the best present: that ever-useful gift of gab.

Behave.

Be bedazzling...
not belligerent.

Behave.

Behave. Be polite—to everyone. Holidays are short. But memories last a long time. So strive to be polite to everyone attending the holiday gathering, no matter if you like them a lot or not much at all. If you respect others, responsible adults can be more likely to act like grown-ups.

Bringing a host or hostess a gift? Simply try to select a gift that matches the recipient's taste. If the person likes a certain color, brand, or flavor, try to customize your present to reflect your attention to his or her particular taste. There's no need to go overboard. The smallest gift is sometimes the most touching and tasteful.

If you would like to bring flowers (a lovely gesture indeed), be sure to provide a vase. If you come bearing loose flowers, the host may end up frantically searching for an empty vase, trimming the stems, and arranging the bouquet while trying to greet other guests. To lessen the stress on your host, you may consider ordering a floral delivery ahead of time.

Be a helpful, gracious, caring guest. Ask if there is anything you can do to help the host or hostess. Offer to assist with either party preparation or dinner clean-up. Most hosts will smile if you offer to remove a few appetizer plates or assist with pouring a drink or two. It doesn't take much energy and the host will be grateful for the gesture. You can reap rewards all year 'round from just a little investment in human kindness at the holidays.

Be bedazzling.

Before you begin holiday visits to family and friends, practice smiling politely, or at least maintaining a pleasant expression on your face. With family functions and foibles, this can be a challenge. But with practice, it's easy to do.

Be charitable with your compliments and kindness. You may not feel the love immediately, but you will reap the benefits later. Your delightful demeanor and agreeable expression can set an upbeat tone for the holiday visiting experience. You may even be complimented for your charming manners! This amicable appearance can be your fallback position should you find yourself in an uncomfortable conversation. No matter what annoys you, just keep on nodding and smiling. Let them wonder what you're thinking.

Don't be belligerent.

Deck the halls, not the guests. Did someone say something that made you less than jolly? Feel more like *throwing* a punch than *drinking* the punch? Take a moment and simmer down. Play nice and "forgettaboutit."

If that's easier said than done, consider these stress reduction strategies:

When you hear thoughtless phrases like: "Nice meeting you. Are you Tom's second or third wife?" or "Exactly what is your natural hair color?" or "You look so different. Have you gained weight?" or the ultimate embarrassing question, "So when is your baby due?" (but you're not pregnant), you might feel a bit uncomfortable, humiliated, or worse yet, you might want sweet verbal revenge. You could be tempted to say a few equally thoughtless, even hurtful, snappy comeback lines. But, stop. Don't drop a dastardly deflection. Roll with it and move on—with grace.

If the other person expresses opinions that are out of line, follow this rule of thumb: don't squabble with a talking turkey! The conversation could end up just an ugly memory and it probably won't make you feel any better. Somewhere I heard that you must keep your words sweet or you might have to eat them later!

Mind your party manners, particularly at holiday time. A holiday party or family affair is not the right occasion to blow off steam. If someone pushes your buttons, control your temper. Focus on being happy, or at least keep busy.

Hint for hot heads: do not raise a hand unless it's to give a toast or help your host!

Keep your thoughts on the bright side.

Embrace holiday seasons as valuable time to improve your relationships and enhance your chances of a "Happy New Year." If you tend to stress over what to say at holiday festivities, here are some suggestions on typically safe conversation topics. In all of the following, be sure to steer clear of heated debates, strong opinions, or controversial remarks that may be associated with them. These are topics that are usually great conversation starters:

◊ Your relationship to the host (family or friend?)
◊ The party venue ("What a beautiful home . . .")
◊ Weather
◊ Hobbies (travel, reading, etc.)
◊ The arts, movies, and theatre

As a rule, while participating in party pleasantries, you can super-size your small talk! But I recommend avoiding the following topics:

◊ Gossip
◊ Health
◊ Politics
◊ Religion
◊ Sex
◊ Tasteless jokes

Good party manners call for your best behavior, so remain in control of your conversation. To maximize your mingle, plan to limit distractions. That includes monitoring your alcohol consumption.

When the party's over . . .

As much fun as a party can be, it's essential to know if the party is supposed to end at a specific time. If so, be sure to respect that time frame. Watch for helpful exit hints. If large groups of partygoers start making tracks toward the door, it is a good sign that they are aware the end is near. You might consider your exit strategy. As gracefully as possible, make your way over to your host and express your gratitude for being included in the holiday fun. Then say, "Cheers, dear!" It's been fun, but you're done. You gotta run.

CHAPTER 15

Writer's Wonderland

Don't Cramp Your Writing Style

E ach year, many of us see this daunting site: a lot of white space on a blank holiday card staring back at you, mocking your lack of time, interest, or imagination. Perhaps you'd like to add more cheer to your holiday cards and letters this year. If so, read on.

Many people choose not to send a personal note in a greeting card. They buy a lovely card with sincere sentiments, but it's in someone else's words.

◊ Okay, I'll give you a couple of points for getting a card.
◊ I'll give you even more points for getting the card to the recipient on time.
◊ But if you want to make a great impression, you may lose points—or get a penalty—for forgetting to make it personal.

No matter whether your message is two words short or two pages long, be sure to include meaningful or inspiring words. No matter how simple or eloquent, you will want to convey that, "You are important to me . . ." or "I am thinking about you." You can relax. There is no hard and fast rule about personal greetings or holiday card messages. The overriding etiquette is simple: your words should be straight from the heart.

Here are a few suggestions designed to help you send the merriest of missives to family, friends, and business colleagues.

Make a list and spell-check it twice.

Check and double-check your card list. Our names are important to us. We want to feel the joy this holiday season, so try your best to pay extra attention and ensure all names are spelled correctly. Does your colleague, Cathy, spell her name with "C" and "y" or with a "K" and an "i"? Believe me, Cathy will appreciate that gift of good manners from you. This careful spelling rule applies to both first and last names and comes from someone who pronounces her name "Diamond" but spells it "Dimond" (that's without an "a").

Size doesn't matter. Thank goodness.

Your card doesn't have to be lengthy, but you can make it heartfelt. If it's a personal card, simply write the way you talk. Your message doesn't have to be mesmerizing, just meaningful. To keep a natural flow, write as if you are on the phone with that person.

Sometimes holiday cards are a bit more formal, and that's appropriate for business relationships. If you are sending a corporate holiday card, be sure you carefully check the pre-printed wording to see if the message conveys your company's or organization's intended holiday cheer. If you write nothing else on the card, that's fine, but at the very least, sign it in your own handwriting.

Happy talk.

Holiday cards are, by design, typically joyful, hopeful, and oftentimes inspirational. Try to spread good wishes or gentle reflections in your cards. Share your joy. If you are inspired to share some tidbits of your terrific year, then do so. Just remember, you can be joyful without being boastful. A few words usually go a long, long way.

Just in case "Yule log-on" this holiday season . . .

Are you considering emailing holiday greetings this year? E-cards can be creative and fun, easy and quick. But be sure to monitor your e-greetings after you send them to ensure that they were not bounced back to you by any of your recipients' computers. Remember, when you email a greeting, you are relying on technology. The holiday season is a time to add some personal touches.

If you can invest the time and energy, consider returning to old-fashioned handwriting. Sit down for a minute and jot down a few words on a holiday greeting card or note. Remember *cursive* handwriting? Yes, that's with a pen . . . on paper. How often do you practice the writing skills you learned in school? Sure, you know you can do it. It's definitely worth it. When someone sees your personal handwriting on a card, that person knows you put forth an extra effort.

What to do if you are prone to phone.

If there's no time or energy in your schedule for writing, mailing, or emailing holiday greetings, or if it just doesn't appeal to you, consider making a few well-placed phone calls. Hearing someone's voice is a wonderful gift. An unexpected, cheerful conversation from a friend is time well spent. If a colleague has had a particularly challenging year, your phone call can help you share your feelings with true emotion and inflection.

If you call and miss someone in real time, then leave a warm message on his or her voicemail. You'll find that your sincere words will be most welcome. We enjoy being remembered during the holidays, no matter whether it's live or on tape.

If you are trying to reach someone with a verbal greeting on his or her cell phone, be extra attentive about your choice of words. Although technology has improved greatly, that cell phone may not be the best place to discuss emotional matters. "Kiss, kiss. Hug, hug. Love ya! Mean it!" That message may be embarrassing if heard by eavesdroppers.

So, writers and communicators, get busy this holiday season. Dole out great doses of unexpected kindness to others through your words and actions. It may be the most precious keepsake you give them.

CHAPTER 16

Your New Year's Solutions Start Today!
Lose the Weight of the Wait

Feel like starting a new year? Why wait? How about today? Any day can be the start of *your* new year and a great time to make resolutions to improve your promote-*ability* and public image. Turn your resolutions into New Year solutions. If you're interested in gaining an impressive impression or captivating communication skills, just keep it simple. It's **E-A-S-Y!**

Dimond's Gems

*Lose your big "but"
and gain a new image.*

First, you must lose your big "but." You may say, "I'm not complaining, *but . . .*" or "Don't think I'm procrastinating, *but . . .*"

Blah, blah, blah. After the big "but," we know you'll go on and on about how hard it'll be to recreate yourself, your image, or your communications confidence. How long do you want to wait? This is so time consuming! A word to the wise: cut out the "but." Consider the word "but" as a big ol' verbal vaporizer just waiting to zap the strength out of your statement. You are hiding behind that big "but" and it's stopping you from playing to your strengths. So lose the weight of the wait! No time to waste. You have a new image to create! It's **E-A-S-Y**!

Ethical behavior: Strive to create and maintain genuine relationships with others. Start with a list of what ethical behaviors you want to exhibit in your new year.

Express yourself appropriately. It's been said that people don't *care* how much you know; they want to know how much you *care*. If you do not care about others, it will soon be evident and you could lose one of the basics of good communications: trust.

Show your delight, determination, and devotion. For instance, maintain eye contact with someone when she or he speaks with you. This doesn't mean you should stare. Simply learn to punctuate your points by looking at someone with a soft glance. Make others feel comfortable and included. While addressing a person by name, give them a polite gaze. Keep in mind, if you give respect, you are more likely to get respect.

Energize! Good communication takes energy. Be sure to reach out and share credit where credit is due. Positive energy usually gets positive feedback. Continue to build your goodwill equity (Remember? It's your credit for doing good things.) among friends, family, colleagues, and coworkers. Of course, if you need to do some damage control—do it! Apologize.

Attitude: Of course, the saying is, "Perception is reality." So for best results, start your new year with a positive attitude!

Act the way you speak. Be consistent in your message and delivery. Be aware of your actions and be clear about your purpose. If you say you will do something, do it. Resist the temptation to make promises you cannot keep. "Acting" interested will not help your positive image if it's just an act. Remember another old saying, "Actions speak louder than words."

Activate your ambition. Go ahead, go for it! Be persistent in obtaining your goals. Envision what you want to achieve and believe in your ability to accomplish it. If you believe in yourself, you have your best chance at success. Remember, accomplishments often take the investment of time.

Style: Be aware of your style, personally and professionally. Show self-confidence in your actions. Unless you respect yourself, others are unlikely to respect you.

Show your self-confidence in your personal style. What "looks good" on another may not be the best choice for you. Be an individual in the way you dress and the way you express yourself. Yet, remember to respect the values and comfort levels of others and adjust your style to respect the occasion.

Share what you know. If you are good at something, share that skill with others. They may be compelled to do the same and you'll end up learning something new, too.

You! Remember to devote time and energy to self-improvement in the new year. Ensure you will have a "Happy New You!"

Yearn to learn. If you are caring and interested in others, they will be more inclined to take an interest in you. When you value someone else's comfort level, your communication improves. Read about other cultures and develop knowledge of the world around you. You will broaden your horizons and become more interesting in the process.

"Yes" should be your answer when you're called upon for volunteering and networking opportunities. Contribute to society and build a network of friends and business colleagues. Be supportive of others, happy with what you're doing, and proud to share your knowledge.

To enhance your public image, put these **E-A-S-Y** New Year's solutions to work each year. You'll be giving yourself a great start for continued positive impressions.

Yoo-hoo! Still reading? If you think this is "The End," think again. It's a beginning. Start your new year—and new *you*—today!

AFTERWORD

Feet up. Music is playing; the Florida breeze, blowing. *Ahhh.* Our breaks are perhaps best appreciated during the busiest times of our lives.

Convention season is in full swing. After hosting two lively conference sessions in Sanibel, I'm taking a break, watching dolphins play in the harbor during a picture-perfect sunset—and I'm smiling. This bittersweet sunset reminds me we must capture life's radiance while we can or we just might miss our chance.

Expand your horizons before the sun sets on you. Share experiences. Meet new people. Do something you haven't tried. You might find you do it well.

You have so much to offer. Pitch your best to the world! Get out there. Play to your strengths. Don't wait until someone tells you to begin.

Don't think, "Why now?" Think, "Why not?"

Capture the joy of living and experiencing *now.* Do it—before the sun sets.

It's game time. Life's a pitch. Have a ball!

ADDITIONAL BOOK ORDERS

I hope you've enjoyed reading *Life's a Pitch!*™. Additional copies can be ordered online, by phone, or fax through the publishing house, Xlibris. It is also available through savvy booksellers. Enjoy!

—*Soni Dimond*

◊ Online: *www1.xlibris.com/bookstore/index.asp*
◊ Email: Orders@xlibris.com
◊ Phone: 888-795-4274 Ext. 276, 24 hours
◊ Fax: 215-599-0114
◊ You are also welcome to contact us at www.sonidimond.com with questions about ordering.

LaVergne, TN USA
20 November 2009
164835LV00002B/103/P